RAISING
fro[m]
INDUSTRY

by
Michael Norton

A Directory of Social Change publication

RAISING MONEY FROM INDUSTRY

by Michael Norton

Cover design by Ruth Lowe

First published in April 1989 by the Directory of Social Change
Radius Works, Back Lane, London NW3 1HL

Typeset by Scarborough Typesetting Services

Printed in Britain by Biddles of Guildford

British Library Cataloguing in Publication Data

Raising money from industry. – 2nd ed.
  1. Great Britain. Charities. Fund raising – Manuals
  I. Norton, Michael, *1942–*
  361.7'0941

  ISBN 0–907164–42–0

Contents

Introduction

The following is the wording of a standard letter of rejection to charitable and other appeals sent out as a pre-printed postcard by George Bernard Shaw to the increasing flow of appeals he received during his lifetime:

> Mr Bernard Shaw receives daily a mass of appeals from charitable institutions, religious sects and Churches, inventors, Utopian writers desirous of establishing international millenial leagues, parents unable to afford secondary education for their children; in short everybody and every enterprise in financial straits of any sort.
>
> All these appeals are founded on the delusion that Mr Shaw is a multi-millionaire. The writers apparently do not know that all his income except hardly enough to meet his permanent engagements is confiscated by the Exchequer and redistributed to those with smaller tax-free incomes, or applied to general purposes by which everyone benefits.
>
> Clearly Mr Shaw's correspondents cannot have his income both ways: in cash from himself and in services from the State. He does not complain of this, having advocated it for more than half a century, and nationalized all his landed property; it is useless to ask him for money: he has none to spare.
>
> He begs to be excused accordingly. No other reply to appeals is possible.

Companies today might express their inability to support the flood of charitable appeals they receive in similar terms.

Like GBS, they are written to by a wide range of people and causes seeking a share of their wealth in the mistaken belief that they have millions to give away. Like GBS, most of the appeals bear little relevance to the ideas, aspirations, or concerns of the donor. Like GBS, such appeals will almost inevitably be rejected.

1

It is true that companies make profits and could, if they so decided, make sizeable charitable contributions out of their profits. But company funds and the profits they earn all belong to the shareholders of the company. The directors of the company are stewards of the company's resources. Their powers are set out in the Memorandum and Articles of Association of the company, and they should at all times act in the interests of the company and its shareholders.

It would be all too easy for the directors or the Chairman to agree to support a particular charitable cause simply because they thought it deserving. But would it be a proper function for them to use the company's funds, rather than dipping into their own pockets, to do this? In the 1960s some larger companies took legal advice on this point and were told that they could make charitable expenditures, but only if they could justify it as being in the interests of the company. If it could not be justified, they might find themselves acting *ultra vires* (beyond their powers).

Today there is less concern about whether company charitable giving is a proper function. The business sector now generally accepts that it is. Shareholders have shown no concern, and on the few occasions where the directors have sought a shareholder resolution to create a charitable budget, this has been passed with overwhelming support. Indeed many shareholders are proud that they have invested in a company which cares, and some companies now cultivate an image of a socially responsible company doing its bit for society and the local communities in which the company operates. And government too calls for private sector involvement in the inner cities, in education, in the environment, in job creation and the promotion of enterprise, and in the arts.

But despite this, companies actually have quite limited funds at their disposal for charitable support, and they use these funds in ways which are quite distinctive. Getting support from a company is quite different from getting support from a grant-making trust, a government or local government agency, or from an individual. Their concerns and interests, the amounts they give, the purposes they give for, the procedures for giving are all different. An applicant charity needs a good understanding of how companies support charity if it is to be successful.

This is particularly the case now that most companies receive literally thousands of appeals a year. A company does not have the resources to support each and every appeal it receives. Nor would it want to. Few appeals are well researched, show any understanding of the company, or are well presented. Even if they are, this will not guarantee success. But it is an important first step to getting support for your cause.

Raising Money from Industry is a basic introduction to company giving. It is one of four books we have produced on the subject. *A Guide to Company Giving*, which is published every second year, provides all the facts and figures on the charitable giving of over 1,300 companies, and a brief statement of the donations policy for every company giving £15,000 or more a year. *Major Companies and their Charitable Giving* provides information in much greater detail on how the top 350 companies spend their community and charitable budgets, as well as describing the company, its business activities, its subsidiaries and its major locations. *The Corporate Donor's Handbook* is a guide to good practice for the company donor, covering everything from setting a budget to how to say no nicely, and is illustrated with many examples of good practice; it also provides the applicant with a detailed picture of what happens from the perspective of the donor.

The aim of this book is to provide basic background information and advice for charities on company giving and the practicalities of getting support. *Part I* covers the background to company giving; who gives, how much they give, in what ways, and for what reasons. It also includes a background briefing on the taxation aspects of company giving. *Part II* discusses the approach, how to identify likely companies, how to write a good application, and how to maximise your chances of success. *Part III* consists of various case studies to illustrate how companies give in practice. It ends with an article from the Allied Dunbar insurance company on how a business can develop a successful community involvement programme (which looks at the process of effective giving from the point of view of the grant-maker).

Each section is written to cover all the main points so that it can be read on its own. This inevitably means that some points are reiterated in a later section, which will serve to reinforce the advice or information that is given. We hope the advice is useful, and that it will help you become more successful in your fund-raising. Good luck!

Michael Norton   January 1989

PART I

BACKGROUND

Company giving

Why companies give

Before sitting down to write an appeal letter, it is useful to have a basic understanding of why companies give. The main reasons can broadly be categorised as follows:

● Companies give to **create goodwill**. They like to be seen as good citizens. Failing to give to anything at all can make a company seem mean spirited. Often a company will tie its level of donations to that of similar companies, not liking to be thought less generous than its peers. It is interesting comparing the level of giving amongst the major banks, insurance companies, oil majors, etc.

● Some companies like to **be associated with certain causes**; this helps their image. For example, a pet food manufacturer will support animal charities, because he wants to be seen as a pet lover not just a profit lover.

● Companies want to **be seen as good neighbours** in the communities where they operate and where they draw their employees from, so they will support local charities.

● Some companies like to **create good relations with employees** through their charitable giving programme. One way of doing this is to support charities that the staff are involved in either as volunteers or in raising money. Some larger companies have formal schemes to donate funds to such charities; others may give some preference, though not necessarily an automatic donation, to charitable appeals proposed by employees.

● Some companies give because they realise that giving is good for them, that it has tangible benefit to the company: some PR benefit from a publicised donation or a more high-profile sponsorship as well as some of the benefits already mentioned. Many of the larger companies recognise these benefits and give out of **enlightened self-interest**.

● Companies may give simply because **it is expected of them**. They receive appeals, and they know that other companies are also receiving appeals which they support. Most companies will also want to support trade charities such as a benevolent fund or an industry research organisation.

● There is a lot of giving on a **knock-for-knock** basis, with company directors soliciting donations for their pet charities (or those of their partners) from their business contacts. This will include friends and colleagues in other companies as well as customers and suppliers. And if they receive support for their cause when they request it, they will be obliged to give support in return when asked.

● Much giving, particularly by smaller companies, is **decided at the top** by the Chairman or Managing Director. Obviously the appeals they personally are interested in will stand a better chance of support. It is true that some large companies do have well-established criteria for their giving; but even then if you can get a friend of the Managing Director to ask on behalf of your cause, you are likely to get a donation, even when it does not exactly fit into those criteria. It always helps to have access at the highest level of a company.

● That brings us into the whole field of the **director's special interest**, where the Managing Director or Chairman or indeed any director uses the charitable budget of the company as an extension of their personal account to fulfil their own charitable commitments. The Americans have coined a term for this phenomenon; they call it the 'incorporated pocketbook'. There is a thin line between the situation where an individual uses his or her interests and beliefs to influence company decisions, and the situation where they use company funds to further their own special interests.

● Some companies give **'because they have always given'**. They see their donations more as an annual subscription, and they will keep a list of the charities they wish to support each year. Your aim, therefore, should be to get your charity's name on to such a list where it exists.

- Sometimes companies give **because the charity persists** in approaching them, and they do not like to keep refusing worthwhile causes. Persistence can pay off. So unless you know the company won't give to your particular cause (and if you can afford the postage), keep trying. A medical charity recently secured a quite substantial donation from a company after more than 10 years of trying. Most charities would not want to continue trying that long in the absence of any positive indication that the company might be prepared to give its support. But if you are turned down you should think a little about whether there is a better way in which you can devise your approach.

It is worth emphasising the sheer chaos of company giving. Few companies have any real policy for their charitable giving. Some admit to this and cover a range of good causes with their limited charitable budget. Some hide what they do behind a wall of secrecy. Some just say that they 'deal with each appeal on its merits'.

Donations and contributions

Under UK company law, a company must declare the donations it makes for charitable purposes in the UK, if these together with any donations it makes for political purposes exceed £200 in any year. [The donations figure will normally appear in the *'Report of the Directors'* section of the Company Annual Report, which is issued to shareholders. This report is usually available to the public on request. If it is not available, it will be filed at Companies' House, where it can be inspected.]

Most companies will simply state a single figure for their charitable donations. Sometimes that figure is qualified or explained, for example:

Donations made to charities *in the UK*

Donations made to charities *in the UK and overseas*

Donations to the *sciences and arts*

............*including a donation of* £00,000 to the Health Promotion Research Trust

............and in addition £00,000 was *donated for educational purposes* (or to *overseas charities*).

There are many other variations.

But companies give their support in more ways than simply making cash donations, which they are obliged to declare. Here are some of the other ways:

● **Gifts in kind**

Companies give their products (anything from paint to packaged holidays), raw materials, offcuts and waste, damaged stock or ends of lines, used equipment, furniture and furnishings. Some of these gifts are of real value. Some are of value to the beneficiary, if not to the donor. Gifts can be made for the charity's own use; or to be turned into cash via an auction, a raffle, a charity shop, or for onward distribution to other charities (as in a Children's Scrap Scheme, or a Goodwill Recycling Workshop).

● **Gifts of services or facilities**

A company can offer such facilities as rooms for meetings, places on training courses, use of a JCB excavator, often at no actual cost to itself.

● **Gifts of staff time and secondment**

A company can help a charity by making available members of its staff who have specialist skills (such as in management, accounting, public relations, promotions, advertising). Such help can be given during company time, or the company might encourage staff to help as volunteers, in their own time. Some larger companies also allow members of staff to work full-time on secondment to charities paying the whole of the employee's costs. A few top companies now believe that the most cost-effective support they can give is in the form of secondment to projects and causes where they wish to make a real impact.

● **Sponsorship**

A donation is a gift for *charitable purposes* whereas sponsorship is a *business expenditure*, bringing a return to the company in the form of public relations, entertainment facilities, welfare facilities for staff, etc. The difference between donations and sponsorship may not always be so clear cut, and is more fully explained in a separate section. Sponsorship support has been increasing fast in recent years, particularly for the arts, but also for conservation and environmental projects and for charity events. A distinction should be drawn between commercial sponsorship on the one hand, which would include much sports sponsorship. This is a proper business expenditure driven by commercial concerns and fully justified in the business return it brings, and would not normally be counted as a 'Community Contribution'. Non-commercial sponsorship on the other hand provides some form of business return, but the community benefit it brings is an equally important motive for the sponsorship.

● **Non-commercial advertising**
Many charities solicit advertising for their annual reports, for brochures produced for special events, and in other printed matter. Most of this advertising could not properly be justified on commercial grounds. It is a convenient way of giving support to a charity, particularly for those companies which have not set up a mechanism for tax-effective company giving. Some companies prefer not to give advertising support, but many do.

● **Support for training**
Many companies are actively and substantially involved in the Youth Training Scheme or Employment Training. Some, like *John Laing* and *Grand Metropolitan*, have established separately consti-tuted companies to handle these training ventures. The cost of company involvement in training schemes is often included as part of the 'total community contributions'.

● **Industry donations**
Most large companies give financial support to a number of industry charities, which are rather different form their main-stream charitable donations. The main recipients of such support are *industry benevolent funds*, which provide support for cases of hardship for employees and former employees of the industry, either in the form of cash hand outs, or by running residential homes. Some industries and some companies may also be supporting their own *research initiatives*. The tobacco industry, for example, supports the Health Promotion Research Trust and *Food Manufacturers* (Mars Confectionery) supports the Mars Health Education Trust.

● **Action for disabled customers**
Most companies carry the cost of providing special facilities for their disabled customers as a normal item of their business expenditure. *British Telecom* is one company that has included these as an item of its community contributions expenditure, perhaps because of the particular importance of telecommuni-

cations in the lives of the disabled and the scale of their involvement.

● **Administrative costs**

Larger companies employ specialist officers or even departments to administer their community contributions. These costs may be included in the total community contributions of the company. *Marks and Spencer*, for example, adopts this practice.

Only a very few companies declare a total community contributions figure. Some may not even know the full extent of the support they give, spread out as it is amongst the Head Office of the company and its plants, branches and subsidiaries and given in the variety of ways described above.

Those companies that are members of the **Per Cent Club** are now being asked to complete an annual return of their support, which categorises their community contributions more or less in the form given above. It is likely that many more of these companies will start to include more details of their support in their Annual Report than a simple donation figure.

Where a total contribution figure is declared alongside a donations figure, the ratio between the two can range from one-to-one for those companies who give all of their support in cash, up to three-to-one, six-to-one or even higher for the very large companies with fully developed community involvement programmes.

The top 20 companies, 1987/88
ranked in order of charitable giving

British Petroleum	£2,900,000
Hanson Trust*	£2,600,000
Marks & Spencers	£2,258,000
TSB Group	£1,920,000
BAT Industries/Allied Dunbar*	£1,900,000
Barclays	£1,863,000
ICI	£1,800,000
National Westminster Bank	£1,651,000
Shell UK	£1,250,000
Van Leer UK	£1,011,000
Unilever	£1,000,000
CIBA-GEIGY	£938,000

Midland Group	£899,000
Gallaher	£841,000
Television South	£825,000
Lloyds Bank	£800,000
RTZ Corporation	£764,000
Esso UK	£763,000
British Telecom	£752,000
J Sainsbury	£700,000

* These companies include in their figure a substantial donation to the Health Promotion Research Trust.

Top 10 community contributors
not all companies declare a figure for total contributions

British Telecom	£11,082,000
National Westminster Bank	£9,700,000
Barclays	£7,306,000
British Petroleum	£5,700,000
Shell UK	£4,600,000
Marks & Spencer	£4,300,000
Midland Bank	£3,635,000
IBM United Kingdom	£3,500,000
Esso UK	£3,000,000
Lloyds Bank	£2,600,000

How much companies give

Every company which makes donations in the UK to charities must declare the total charitable donations it has made during the year, if these together with any political donations have exceeded £200. This statement is normally included in the Director's Report contained within the company annual report.

This figure provides the base data for calculating how much companies give. A word of warning first. Not all companies declare their charitable donations figure on the same basis. Some simply do not have to hand information on the often quite small donations made by subsidiaries and local branches. Some include overseas donations in addition to their UK donations. Some include 'special' donations which, although made to a charity, are made really for business purposes, whilst others specifically exclude these special donations. Examples of special donations include the donation to the Thalidomide Children's Trust made by *Distillers* (now part of *Guinness*) which was part of the settlement of claims made by affected families, the donations by tobacco companies to the Health Promotion Research Trust, which is an industry-sponsored body on health matters including the effects of smoking (the brewers have a similar charity dealing with alcohol). Then there is the difference between 'charitable donations' and 'community contributions', which was discussed on *page 9*, and some companies make available only a figure for their total contribution, which includes sponsorship, advertising support, support for enterprise, secondment, in-kind support as well as cash donations.

Simply adding up the figures will not yield a precise figure for either cash contributions or total contributions. There is inevitably a large element of guesswork in trying to estimate the total. Our best estimate for the support given by companies to charity in 1987 is as follows:

Cash donations to UK charities	£135,000,000
Sponsorship of the arts and goods causes (*amount received by charity*)	£35,000,000
Support in cash, kind and secondment to enterprise agencies	£20,000,000
Advertising in charity brochures	£20,000,000
Joint promotions (*amount received by charity*)	£20,000,000
Secondment of company staff (excluding enterprise agencies)	£5,000,000
Gifts in kind	£25,000,000
Total support by companies	**£250,000,000**

The figures for sponsorship and joint promotions are estimates of the amounts actually received by charities, rather than the cost to the company, which includes promotional costs benefiting the company rather than the charity. The figures for brochure advertising and gifts in kind are complete guesses, and could wildly underestimate the support given, especially since there are no figures for the very large amount of informal support that is given.

More reliable figures are available for the support for charities from other sources:

Grant-making trusts	£400,000,000
Central government	£280,000,000
Manpower Services Commission (Training Agency)	£560,000,000
Housing Corporation	£815,000,000
Arts Council	£130,000,000
Other official support	£30,000,000
Local authorities	£550,000,000
Tax reliefs on investment and covenant income	£600,000,000
Rate reliefs	£145,000,000
Legacies	£400,000,000

Note: These figures relate to 1987. They do not include individual giving through fund-raising, subscriptions, covenants and donations. The figure for the *Manpower Services Commission* covers various programmes, but the Commission has now been succeeded by the *Training Agency*, and some programmes have been substantially altered or even terminated, so that figures for subsequent years may not continue at this level. In 1988 *telethon fund-raising* came into its own, and the amount raised by such events as Children in Need, Telethon '88 and Comic Relief together with other broadcast appeals amounted to well over £100,000,000.

The comparison of company giving with charitable support from other sources shows how *relatively small* the company contribution is. Yet it is an *important* contribution and a *useful additional source* of income for charities.

Has company giving been growing?

An analysis of the figures over the past years shows the top 200 companies having given £63.3 million in 1987, and this compares with donations as shown in the table on the next page for the previous 8 years adjusted for inflation:

	£ million donations	% of pre-tax profits
1987	63.3	0.20
1986	60.8	0.22
1985	49.8	0.20
1984	49.3	0.18
1983	41.2	0.21
1982	40.0	0.24
1981	37.4	0.21
1980	42.0	0.19
1979	39.7	0.18

Although this shows a rising trend in terms of the total donated and a fairly stable pattern for the percentage of profits applied for charitable purposes, the figures need qualifying. Companies declare their giving on different bases, and this can affect the picture. For example, *Hewlett Packard* reported a figure of £1.1 million for the total of its community support in 1986, whereas the figure given in 1987 of £169,000 represented only the cash support given by the company. Another important consideration is the large number of takeovers and mergers that have taken place in recent years. The effect of this is to increase the donations of the top 200 companies as they swallow up each other or smaller companies, absorbing the donations function of the companies taken over. *BAT industries*, for example, now includes the donations of *Allied Dunbar*, *Eagle Star* and *Wiggins Teape*, all of which had been substantial donors. This means that it is quite difficult to say anything meaningful about the rate of increase in company charitable giving.

There are, however, two noticeable trends in recent years. Firstly the giving by the leading companies appears to have reached something of a plateau. Secondly, in the middle range of companies, there are a significant number of companies which have increased their donations budgets very substantially.

There are also a few companies that have reduced their donations significantly. The move from covenant giving to single payment giving made possible by the 1986 Finance Act now allows a greater volatility in company giving. It allows companies to increase their tax-exempt donations in any year without having to make a forward commitment to similar increases in future years. It also allows companies to reduce their giving for whatever reason. Although the number of companies which have reduced their donations very substantially has been quite small, the implication for the future is that if company profits come under pressure, charitable expenditure which is always a peripheral expenditure for the company could feel the pinch.

Per Cent Giving

Company giving is normally related to company pre-tax profits as a measure of company generosity, for it is out of company profits that company donations are made.

What is a reasonable percentage of profits for companies to give?

Here are some possibilities

0%

Since the company belongs to its shareholders, it is the shareholder's funds which are being given away as charitable donations. Some companies believe that the responsibility for charitable giving should belong to the shareholders themselves, and not to the company acting on their behalf. These companies see their job as to generate profits and pay good dividends to shareholders. It would then be a matter for shareholders as to how to spend their dividend income – and whether to give to charity. This is a perfectly rational viewpoint for a company. It does not mean that the company is ungenerous, only that it does not see company giving as a proper company function.

0.2%

This appears to be the average for larger companies in the UK. Company giving has fluctuated around this level for many years. During the second half of the 1980s company profits have been growing quite rapidly, and there has been a real growth in the charitable support given by companies in the UK. It is obviously worth looking out for those companies that are 'doing well' where one would expect to see a rapid profit growth matched by a rapid growth in charitable donations.

0.5%

In December 1986, a **Per Cent Club** was launched to encourage companies to contribute one-half-of-one-per-cent of their profits in community contributions (or alternatively 1% of dividend payments to shareholders). Over 175 companies have now joined the Club. But two points should be noted: Firstly, community contributions include more than just charitable donations; contributions would cover a good cause sponsorship, gifts in kind, secondments, etc. Secondly, the percentage that member companies are expected to give is a percentage of *UK profits*, not of total profits. Some companies, such as Glaxo, earn most of their profits overseas, whilst others, such as British Telecom, operate almost wholly within the UK. Based on this wider definition, most companies in membership of the Club would have been giving at around or even above the half per cent level anyway. Consequently the Per Cent Club will not lead to any dramatic increase in company giving in the immediate term, but set a benchwork for other companies to emulate, and tie member companies' contributions to profit or dividend levels.

1%

The original intention of the Per Cent Club was for companies to contribute one per cent of their profits, and this remains a target for the Club. If this were to be achieved, it would lead to a substantial rise in company giving. One per cent is a nice round figure. It still means that 99% of company profits will be available to shareholders or to plough back into the business. There are companies which have formally committed themselves to the one per cent level, including for example, *United Biscuits* (one per cent in community contributions) and *A Goldberg* (one per cent in donations).

2%

Two per cent appears to represent 'best practice in the UK, although only a small handful of companies give at or near this level. In the United States, the '*President's Task Force on Private Sector Initiatives*' recommended the two per cent level as a target for corporate public involvement in the US. A further basis for this level is the Per Cent Club movement in the US, where around 1,000 companies across the United States have now committed themselves to giving 2% of pre-tax profits to the community. Although the US situation is markedly different – both in the role of statutory authorities and in the funding of important areas such as health and higher education – what happens in the US does provide a stimulus for UK companies. Ten years ago, per cent giving would not have been achievable in the UK; in ten years' time, perhaps 2% won't seem unrealistic.

5%

Alongside the Two Per Cent Clubs in the US, there are also Five Per Cent Clubs often with a surprisingly large number of members.

10%

Ten per cent is the level of 'tithing'. It is also the maximum level permitted under US tax law for US corporations. In Birmingham, Alabama, there is a Ten Per Cent Club with two members.

100%

In the UK there is no theoretical limit to the amount a company can give. Indeed, some companies have been specially set up to earn money for particular charities. Usually these enterprises are closely linked to the charity (for example, a gift shop at a museum, or a Christmas

Card operation for a national charity). But there is nothing to stop any UK company from deciding to give all or a substantial part of its profits to charity (provided that its shareholders agree with this!).

What companies support

We sent out a questionnaire asking companies to indicate their grant-making preferences. We have analysed the response for a sample of 100 companies. This gives a reasonable indication of current preferences in company grant-making.

1. Preferred Areas

We asked companies if they gave preference to the following particular areas of work. The following were the preferences shown:

Children and youth	58%
Medical	54%
Social welfare	36%
Education	35%
Enterprise and training	26%
The arts	22%
Overseas aid and development	7%
Other	9%

In 'other' category companies were asked to give any areas of preference other than those listed. In this category companies indicated preferences for the elderly, heritage, environment, local events. The survey was carried out just before the current concern with the environment triggered off by Mrs Thatcher's speech at the Royal Society of Arts in Autumn 1988. Had we included an environment category and done a follow up survey, it is likely that a reasonable proportion of companies would give some preference to environmental causes.

2. Exclusions

We asked companies which types of appeal they did **not** normally support. The results were as follows:

Local appeals not in areas of company presence	85%
Purely denominational (religious) appeals	78%
Circular appeals	73%
Advertising in charity brochures	73%
Appeals from individuals	71%
Overseas projects	66%
Large national appeals	53%
Fund raising events	48%
Other stated exclusions	4%

Most companies are unwilling to support local appeals with no local relevance or connection to the company. There is a strong dislike for circular appeals, which shows how worthwhile it is to take the effort to send a personally written appeal to a company (if it is word processed, it should not appear to be so). Many companies feel that the money paid for brochure advertising is more likely to end up in the hands of a printer or a promotion agent rather than the charity, and prefer to make a direct donation; on the other hand, many smaller companies can be persuaded to take brochure advertising, and some larger companies do have budgets for this form of support. Most public companies will not support purely denominational appeals because they do not feel that this is appropriate; however projects which benefit a wider public but are run by denominational charities are more likely to be supported.

It is interesting to see how many companies (over half the sample) say that they prefer not to support large national appeals. They feel that the small support they can give will not be significant alongside the millions that can be raised from the public and larger grant-making bodies. What companies say and what they do in the face of persistent and high powered fund-raising may in fact differ, and many of the companies which said that they excluded large national appeals probably did support the Wishing Well Appeal for Great Ormond Street Hospital, *because they felt they had to*. Large national charities can, of course, ask for support for specific projects or expenditures.

Another less popular area was for overseas projects. Only 7% gave this as a stated preference, whereas 66% stated it as an exclusion. Overseas projects are more likely to be supported if the company has some connection with that country, when support may be given through local subsidiaries or the international HQ budget. Most companies also feel that the disaster emergency appeals are 'large', 'national' and likely to be supported by individual donors (including their employees).

3. Other points

57% of companies said that they did not welcome unsolicited appeals. This could be because they only supported causes known to the Chairman or Managing Director. Or it could be because they wanted to warn off intending applicants in order to reduce the volume of appeal mail, which is often too large to handle with comfort. On the other hand, if you do not send an appeal, you are highly unlikely to get *unsolicited support*.

80% of companies gave some preference to local charities situated in the communities in which they have a presence. The donations may often be smaller than for national grants. A significant minority of companies said that they now *only* gave to local charities.

52% of companies gave preference to appeals 'relevant to their business'. There is a considerable latitude for interpreting this, and it is up to applicant charities to show companies how their appeal is relevant.

33% of companies said that they gave preference to appeals in which a member of staff was involved. A few of the very large companies have formal procedures for matching employee involvement. It can never harm an appeal to show that a member of staff is involved with the charity, and encouraging employee involvement has been one of the noticeable trends of the late 1980s.

Current trends in company giving

Company giving is quite unlike trust giving, and a good understanding of why companies give and their changing priorities for charitable support will be helpful for grant-seekers.

1. Company giving has become more volatile

Although company giving has been growing in real terms, it has been growing largely in line with company profits. Over the past 8 years, as has been shown, the major companies have continued to donate around one fifth of one per cent of their pre-tax profits to charitable causes on average. There has been a remarkable consistency in this figure from year to year for companies as a whole.

However, particularly for smaller companies, there has been a greater volatility from year to year. During a period of rising profits, these sudden changes have, with a few exceptions, tended to go upwards. But, should company profits begin to fall, there is the scope for donations to be cut equally rapidly.

What has made this possible is the 1986 Finance Act which for the first time allowed companies to make one-off donations to charity tax-effectively, without having to commit themselves via a Deed of Covenant to giving similar amounts over a period of four years.

Some of the changes have been quite staggering. Between 1986 and 1987, the giving by *J Rothschild Holdings* jumped from £18,000 to £250,000; and of *Rosehaugh* from £18,000 to £92,000 between 1987 and 1988. Here are two companies which have grown rapidly in recent years and now decided to establish a proper and substantial charity presence. Two other examples are *British Telecom*, which has grown from £489,000 in 1987 to £752,000 in 1988, and to over £1 million in 1989, and *British Airways*, which has grown from £38,000 in 1986 to £86,000 in 1987. These are both large privatisation companies, which once having emerged into the public arena, then begin to establish a community affairs budget on an appropriate scale. Other companies increasing their donations substantially might be companies doing rather well, companies strongly supporting the present government line that the private sector ought to be doing more for the community, and companies which are keen to support particular government initiatives (such as City Technology Colleges).

This means that vigilance could pay dividends. Watch out for companies coming of age (*Amstrad* reported no donations in 1987 and *Eurotunnel* was too new to have produced an annual report by 1988). Watch out for privatisation stocks, past and future (the *electricity industry*, including local electricity boards, the *water authorities*), and for bodies grooming themselves for an eventual flotation (the *building societies*). Watch out for companies and industry sectors doing rather well (in 1988, a number of larger car dealerships, independent TV contractors, promotional and advertising agencies, for example, began to appear in the lists of leading donors). Watch out for the known government supporters (for example, Sir Hector Laing's *United Biscuits* raised its donations from £157,000 in 1986 to £415,000 in 1987). Watch out for new members of the Per Cent Club who commit themselves to giving over half of one per cent of pre-tax profits to the community, where perhaps they may be having to raise their contribution substantially to meet this commitment (this club now has 175 members which it hopes to raise to 250 by 1990). At the same time, watch out for companies having a bad year, who might then decide to make a substantial reduction in their contribution.

2. A growing professionalism

Certainly with the larger companies, a much more professional approach is being adopted towards the business of giving money away. Many of the very large companies have established community affairs departments. Some are beginning to recruit from the voluntary sector (for example, Catherine Graham-Harrison of *Citicorp* had previously worked for a housing association), some take advice from outside advisors (for example, Sir Geoffrey Wilson, the former Chairman of Oxfam and of the Race Relations Board, advises *Allied Dunbar Assurance* on aspects of their charitable policy).

Even for those who have been internally promoted, there is much more information, training, and mutual discussion. The *Corporate Responsibility Group* and *Business in the Community* run regular meetings for community affairs personnel. There is now an infrastructure of organisations active in promoting community involvement including *Business in the Community* (company community involvement), *Action Match* (sponsorship), *Association for Business Sponsorship of the Arts* (arts sponsorship), the *Volunteer Centre* (employee community involvement). These organisations all produce newsletters or magazines, which also serve to keep those in the voluntary sector up to date.

3. A more selective approach

All companies now receive many more appeals than they can possibly hope to support. Very large companies such as *Marks and Spencer* and the High Street banks now calculate that they receive some 30,000 appeals annually in total at head office and local branches.

This imposes a severe administrative burden, particularly for those larger companies that have no clearly defined charitable policy and no specialist staff administering charitable appeals. These companies will be considering 'each appeal on its merits', and having to make almost instant decisions on which appeals to reject without further consideration. Most companies now reject out of hand circular appeals, poorly presented appeals or appeals which are obviously inappropriate. It is for this reason that applicants are advised to think carefully whether the company might be interested before approaching a company, to write a personal appeal letter, and to highlight in that letter the reasons why the company might like to give its support. The letter should be short and to the point. Imagine someone having to read 60 appeals a week and only able to devote two or three hours a week to appeals administration (this would be typical for a company with no specialist appeals staff); the easier you make it for them to read and respond to your appeal, the easier it will be for them to say yes.

Many more companies, though still a minority, are responding to the growing level of appeals by developing an appeals policy, selecting those areas which they particularly wish to support, and making this information publicly available. It is important to get as much information as you can about the company first. Some companies publish a special report on their charitable policies, some print anything from a few lines to a few pages in the company annual report, and all larger companies are covered in the book *'Major Companies and their Charitable Giving'*. Even here, it is worth giving some thought to your appeal, for many companies feel that charities simply find out the appeals policy and adapt their request accordingly.

4. Themes and issues

Companies have different concerns and interests from other grant-makers. One major priority for company support in the 1980s has been support for employment training and enterprise. This support has largely been channelled into *local enterprise agencies* and *Business in the Community*. But some companies have made very major commitments to small grants or loan funds for small or new businesses, and to the creation of managed workspace in former industrial or commercial premises. Some support has gone to selected charities favoured by the business sector, such as *Project Fullemploy* and the *Prince's Youth Business Trust*. Companies have seen that they have a major role to play in economic regeneration and in the inner cities, and have sought to provide support for this on a quite substantial scale.

More recently, there has been a focus on education, particularly in relation to *School-Industry Links* following Industry Year in 1986, and in technology, which goes far beyond support for City Technology Colleges. Organisations such as *Young Enterprise* and *local education compacts* have benefited.

What will the trends be for the 1990s? Issues relating to the expected shortages of skilled staff and school leavers, such as training and day care? Issues relating to changing population trends in general and the ageing of the population, in particular, such as support for carers and care in the community? Health?

The environment? New trends can be spotted if you keep a close eye on what is happening.

5. Donations are not everything

Companies, unlike other charitable donors, can make much more available than just cash. Things, services, people, expertise can also be made available, often at much less cost than a cash donation. Some companies now believe that the major contribution they can make is through secondment of their staff, possibly backed up by donations of equipment to selected causes. For companies such as *Pilkington* and *IBM*, their cash giving now represents only a tiny proportion of their community involvement activity. The consequence of this is that charities have to be alert to the opportunities that exist for non-cash support.

Another development is in the field of sponsorship. In the late 1970s, companies began to sponsor the arts, and this support grew from virtually nothing in 1977 to some £30 million by 1987. Sponsorship offers benefits both ways, to the sponsor and the recipient. It normally also involves a bigger financial commitment. In the mid-1980s sponsorship was being extended to conservation projects, with a lead being taken by the *World Wide Fund for Nature*, and to local community projects, where the London Borough of Newham-based charity, *Community Links*, has pioneered the development of this by setting up *Action Match* in 1989 as an advisory service to promote the opportunities for social sponsorship to business and to charities.

Since companies have far larger budgets for promotion, publicity, corporate and brand advertising than they do for charitable donations, it makes good sense for charities to think about the possibilities of sponsorship and other joint promotions.

Another large company budget is for staff welfare. Here again there are opportunities. Many charities are professional welfare agencies with skills, knowledge and products which might be helpful to a company. An alcohol education charity or an AIDS counselling charity both have important roles to play in helping companies develop sensible policies and providing services to employees. The same principle could be extended to welfare rights, citizens' advice, and on a completely different tack, a US organisation dealing with young addicts put on courses for retail executives on 'Shop-lifting – techniques and prevention' using the undoubted (former) expertise of the young people in its care!

The point is that charitable giving is often quite a marginal activity, and that companies can support charities in a variety of other ways. These opportunities will develop as companies and charities become aware of the different ways they can work together.

Secondment

One way in which charities can receive substantial help from companies is through having a member of the company's staff working for the charity *on secondment* from the company. The secondee continues to receive full remuneration from the company during the period of the secondment, whilst the charity is responsible for paying any additional costs connected with the post – such as supervision, incidental expenditure, project costs.

Some large companies will be spending a considerable part of their community affairs budget on secondment. For companies such as *Pilkington*, *Prudential* and *United Biscuits*, the cost to the company of its secondment programme will be at least as great as the cost of its charitable donations. However, secondment is largely confined to the very large companies with well developed community affairs programmes.

The cost of a secondment to the company will be around £30,000 per secondee per year (or pro-rata for shorter term or part-time secondments). There are probably 500–700 company staff working in the voluntary sector on secondment, although the greater proportion of these will be working with Local Enterprise Agencies and in the fields of economic development, training and employment projects, rather than with traditional charities.

Companies receive far more requests for secondees than they can satisfy, so it is important for those seeking a secondee to be aware of how, why and when companies decide to make a secondment before making a request.

Types of secondment

Although secondment is usually thought of as a full-time arrangement, it can in fact take many forms:

● **Part-time,** involving perhaps a few hours a week.

This might include getting company executives to serve on a Management Committee where they can bring new perspectives and skills. One such scheme is *Lawyers in the Community* where a dozen major law firms have agreed to sit on charity committees, mainly in Tower Hamlets, Southwark and Spitalfields; this initiative is co-ordinated by the Action Resource Centre.

It also includes business advisers working with enterprise agencies and youth enterprise schemes, who will make themselves available to provide specialist advice and possibly some training on an 'as needed' basis.

● **Project assignments or 'missions'**

Here the secondee provides an input to solve a problem or do a specific piece of work. Such arrangements are usually quite short-term and possibly part-time.

Many advertising agencies are happy to design a logo, a brochure or even a promotional campaign on this basis. For example, *Saatchi and Saatchi* have a formal procedure for applying for 'free help'.

Two local store management staff from *Marks and Spencer* in Leicester worked with a goodwill furniture recycling workshop for a total of 100 hours over 3 months to devise practical ways of increasing the supply of furniture for renovation.

Occasionally, projects are undertaken by trainee staff as part of their training. Providing that there is proper supervision, such an arrangement can be wholly satisfactory. For example, on Merseyside, a local Gingerbread group with salary scale problems had a job evaluation study undertaken by a *British Telecom* graduate personnel trainee.

These are just a few examples of the possibilities of project assignments. They may be far easier to arrange than a longer term secondment. You know what you need done, you know the skills needed to do the work and where they might be found, you can approach a company able to give the support you need, and it does not involve a big expense. Indeed, if carried out after hours on a volunteer basis, it will cost the company nothing.

● **Longer-term secondments**

Full-time secondments are normally made for a period from a few months up to two years. These may involve younger high fliers, as part of a management development programme, those in mid-career needing to 'recharge their batteries', or those in the run up to retirement (which will be discussed separately).

A full-time secondment is a substantial commitment by the company to the charity, so it must be to a charity which the company really wants to support. The company should feel that the arrangement will provide some positive and longer-lasting achievement, and where possible the arrangement should be beneficial to all parties (the charity, the company and the secondee).

There are many examples of long-term secondments by companies, and the case study of the *Prudential* shows how this works in practice from the company's standpoint.

It should be noted that not only companies can make secondments. Secondments to charities have been organised from local authorities and government departments. Equally, some companies have seconded staff to public bodies and as government advisers.

● **Pre-retirement secondment**

The period before retirement provides good opportunities for secondment, either as an alternative to early retirement, or as a transfer to a new post-retirement 'career' as a charity volunteer. Some companies, notably the big banks, have a formal programme of pre-retirement secondment.

One example of how this can work is the *British Telecom* employee who worked two days a week for a County Association for the Disabled, undertaking a feasibility study on establishing a new centre. After retirement, the secondee continued to work with the Association as a volunteer.

There is a vast pool of talent, experience and skills amongst the retired, and involvement in working for a charity during the run up period is one good way of making good use of this. There are also schemes such as **REACH** (the Retired Executive Action

Clearing House, 89 Southwark Street, London SE1 0HD) and **The Emeritus Register** (1st Floor, Quadrant Arcade Chambers, Romford RM1 3EH), which seek to encourage volunteering after retirement.

The benefits of secondment

For the charity, the value of a secondment is an additional pair of hands provided free, and more important, someone with specialist knowledge, skills and aptitudes.

But this would not be a satisfactory relationship if the benefits were only one-sided. The seconder and the secondee must also get something out of the arrangement.

The benefits to the secondee are a chance to work in a new environment, perhaps to learn new skills and to extend horizons. Working away from the often highly-structured environment of a company can promote initiative, provide creative challenges, give the employee knowledge of problems and situations which might be useful on re-entry into the company, and increase personal effectiveness.

For the company, the benefits include the personal development of a valued employee, goodwill and other public relations benefits, the acquisition of specialist knowledge and experience by the company (of the cause or area being tackled by the charity), and benefits within the employee structure of the company – these could include the removal of promotion blockages, a move to a new career on retirement for pre-retirement secondees, or the chance to move sideways into the voluntary sector for executives who would otherwise become redundant.

How to obtain and manage a secondee

The Action Research Centre has produced a booklet entitled *Getting the Best from Secondment* which is a detailed guide to secondment, obtaining a secondee and managing the secondment. The following good practice summary outlines the main practical points to bear in mind:

1. Analyse your own organisation to establish if there is a real need for a secondee.

2. Draw up a short policy statement outlining why secondment is considered appropriate for your organisation and why you wish to develop a partnership with other sectors. Ensure this is accepted by your management committee and relevant staff.

3. Continue to pursue other options towards meeting the need.

4. Decide which organisation would be the most likely source of supply.

5. Establish what resources you have available to support a secondee and decide who would manage the secondment.

6. Draw up a detailed job description and person specification (complete ARC Request Form if using ARC as a broker) but remain flexible.

7. Select a secondee with the same care as you would an employee; allow opportunity for a potential secondee to visit your organisation several times.

8. Ensure that all parties clearly understand what each seeks from the secondment.

9. Agree objectives for the secondment with the secondee and seconding organisation.

10. Ensure that written agreements between the parties before the secondment begins cover:

(a) A job description and objectives.

(b) The period of secondment, including start and finish dates.

(c) Terms and conditions of employment as they apply to the secondee (for instance, salary, pay increase policy, benefits, holidays, hours of work and overtime arrangements; usually these will be unaltered and in any case the secondee should not be worse off)

(d) Insurance arrangements.

(e) Company car, secondee's car, or no car.

(f) Expenses relating to any extra travelling to work.

(g) Expenses and class of travel (unless specified otherwise you are responsible for out-of-pocket expenses during the conduct of a secondee's business).

(h) Procedures for dealing with conflicts of interest, confidentiality and business practice issues.

(j) Probation and notice of termination, if applicable.

(k) A statement as to whether wider resources of the seconding organisation are to be made available.

(l) The identification of clear communication channels between all parties, agreeing the key contacts in the seconding body and your organisation.

(m) Procedures for performance appraisal.

(n) Return arrangements (if applicable) including debriefing processes.

11. Arrange a carefully planned induction programme, and be prepared to spend time with the new secondee.

12. Monitor and appraise the performance of the secondee at regular intervals to ensure maximum effectiveness, conforming to the seconding organisation's requirements as necessary.

13. Encourage the secondee to maintain contact with the seconding organisation or do so yourself.

14. Take appropriate opportunities to publicise the secondment and the seconding organisation's contribution.

15. Ensure that the return arrangements are discussed well in advance, and that adequate debriefing takes place.

16. After the secondment, evaluate the benefits for all parties.

17. Keep in touch with the secondee and seconding organisation afterwards.

The Action Resource Centre

ARC is a national voluntary organisation which transfers business skills and resources to community organisations. It gives priority to addressing the needs of disadvantaged inner city and urban communities in the UK. It promotes secondment by companies and encourages good practice. It acts as a broker matching requests for secondment to opportunities. ARC also promotes the transfer of other resources via its Business Links Scheme, Lawyers in the Community, Community Accountancy and management training in the community. ARC works through a network of area offices supported by a London head office. Addresses are as follows:

ARC HEAD OFFICE
Secondment Programmes Unit, CAP House, 3rd Floor, 9–12 Long Lane, London EC1A 9HD. Tel: 01-726 8987.

ARC AVON
c/o Sun Life Assurance Society plc, 5th Floor, St Lawrence House, 29/31 Broad Street, Bristol BS1 2JE Tel: 0272-221144.

ARC GREATER LONDON
CAP House, 3rd Floor, 9–12 Long Lane, London EC1A 9HD. Tel: 01-726 8987.

ARC GREATER MANCHESTER
111 The Piazza, Piccadilly Plaza, Manchester M1 4AN. Tel: 061-3391.

ARC HUMBERSIDE PROJECT OFFICE
c/o Hull Area Office, Advice Centre, 24 Anlaby Road, Hull HU1 2PA. Tel: 0482-27266.

ARC LEICESTERSHIRE
The Business Advice Centre, 30 New Walk, Leicester LE1 6TF. Tel: 0533-554464.

ARC MERSEYSIDE
c/o Premier Brands UK Ltd, Pasture Road, Moreton, Wirral, Merseyside L46 8SE. Tel: 051-678 8888.

ARC NORTHERN IRELAND
ARC House, Enterprise Centre, 103/107 York Street, Belfast BT15 1AB. Tel: 0232-328000.

ARC NOTTINGHAMSHIRE
6th Floor, City House, Maid Marian Way, Nottingham NG1 6BH. Tel: 0602-470749/470839.

ARC WEST MIDLANDS
1st Floor, Cornwall House, 31 Lionel Street, Birmingham B3 1AP. Tel: 021-200 2363.

ARC WEST YORKSHIRE
c/o British Rail Eastern Region, 1 Aire Street (room 101), Leeds LS1 4PR. Tel: 0532-458132.

ARC's priorities and criteria

When considering requests from projects and organisations, ARC gives priority to intiatives contributing to community development in inner city areas of the UK and dealing with one or more of the following:

(a) Social conditions (e.g. combating drug or alcohol abuse, developing opportunities for disadvantaged groups, supporting self-help).

(b) Economic conditions (e.g. stimulating work opportunities, education and training for work, alternatives to unemployment, recycled resources).

(c) The urban environment (e.g. renovation of buildings, conservation).

Criteria for project assistance

In deciding whether it is able to assist your particular organisation or project ARC also takes into account the extent to which it:

(a) Meets an identified need and does not duplicate the work of
other bodies.

(b) Emphasises and fosters self-help and independence in the
community or client group it is serving.

(c) Reflects local needs and makes a local contribution.

(d) Is able to demonstrate charitable objectives (the organisation
will usually, but not always, be a registered charity).

(e) Can provide appropriate support (e.g. induction, management, accommodation, expenses).

(f) Can provide a suitable opportunity for a secondee (i.e. likely
to bring benefits to all parties).

(g) Is committed to equal opportunities, and is without party
political bias.

(h) Falls within the geographical area covered by ARC.

How the Prudential seconds

The *Prudential Corporation* is a major UK insurance, financial
services and property services company. It states that it has 'long
acknowledged that it has a responsibility to return to the
community a proportion of the wealth it draws from it', and that
'doing good deeds and creating good will go hand in hand'. Each
year it spends some £350,000 on charitable donations and as
much or more again on secondment. These resources are
channelled largely into supporting health care, social welfare,
education, youth, jobs and enterprise, training and heritage,
which the Prudential has defined as its priority areas. At any one
time some 16 members of staff are out on secondment. These are
spread around the country, reflecting the geographical presence
of the Prudential, but managed from Head Office. Secondments
have been made to organisations as diverse as The Dystonia
Society, Harrogate Volunteers Centre, Opportunities for the

Disabled, and Merseyside Education Training and Enterprise (METEL). Because the cost of a two-year secondment can amount to anything from £40,000 to £70,000, there is an enormous responsibility on the company to show that there is a return for this outlay. This return is seen partly as an investment in contributing to a socially worthwhile cause, and partly in the benefit it brings to the performance of the secondee and any return to the company. Although the charity will be looking for specific skills and activities, the Prudential feels that the job specification should be balanced one-third to what the employee can do and two-thirds towards providing new experiences, opportunities and challenges which will contribute to the secondee's own development.

All Prudential secondees are volunteers who have been interviewed internally and personally selected before being offered to the organisation as a secondee. Secondment is not seen as an alternative to retirement or redundancy. The Secondment Manager will select those causes that the company is prepared to support and advertise the job description internally. She then conducts a first interview with the receiving organisation. In selecting the organisations to support, the following criteria are used:

1. The company examines the organisation and decides whether it would want to be associated with it. This is done in much the same way as donations decisions are taken.

2. The company satisfies itself that the organisation understands why it needs a secondee – what the secondment will achieve and what sort of person with what skills and abilities is needed to undertake the tasks. There is a preference for supporting secondments which will clearly allow the organisation to move forward in some substantial way in order to create lasting achievements. Secondments which are requested simply to provide a free body will not be supported.

3. The company identifies a suitable person who is agreeable to working on secondment. A good secondment requires the right secondee.

4. The company then discusses the practical arrangements, the nature of the job, the tasks to be undertaken, and how the secondment will be managed and supervised in order to ensure that all parties benefit.

5. The company satisfies itself that the arrangement will work. It normally will require regular reporting and appraisal, the establishment of personal objectives for the secondee at the outset, and adequate induction, training and support to be provided by the organisation to allow the secondee to perform.

6. Since one of the company's objectives is the creation of goodwill, proper acknowledgement of the support and due publicity is welcomed.

The initial approach will normally be in writing. This should involve a presentation in sufficient detail to allow the company to decide that the proposal is worth pursuing further.

Sponsorship

Sponsorship is an increasingly important form of company support. By matching opportunities for giving support with specific needs or tangible benefits that the sponsor might obtain for his company, a relationship very different from that of a donor and supplicant emerges. It is clearly a satisfactory arrangement for many companies, as the very rapid growth in sponsorship expenditure in recent years evidences. Arts sponsorship has grown from practically nothing a decade ago, to some £30 million annually today, according to estimate produced by ABSA, the **Association for Business Sponsorship of the Arts**.

Increasingly sponsorship is spilling over from the arts into other areas of charitable endeavour. There is now a well established market for sponsorship of conservation of environmental and wildlife schemes, and a number of agencies provide sponsorship opportunities in this area for industry – in particular the **World Wildlife Fund**, the **Groundwork Foundation** and **UK 2000** (details of these organisations are given in the list of helpful organisations at the end of this section).

Charities in other fields have been slower to see the possibilities that sponsorship might offer in their quest for funds. It is not confined to the sponsorship of charity events, such as entertainments and other fund-raising activities, or to the sponsorship of publications, where the donor's name can be attached. The potential is much wider than this, both at a national and at a local level.

The sponsorship of a campaign designed to reduce the incidence of hypothermia amongst elderly people in the town where it has a presence, for example, might be a more than satisfactory alternative for a company than scattering its donations budget over a wider range of activities in small amounts. This sort of sponsorship can bring credit and good publicity to the sponsor, as well as achieve something tangible and substantial. *Shell UK*, one of the leaders in the field of sponsorship, sponsors a nationwide 'Village Ventures' competition with Rural Community Councils; *National Westminster Bank* provides money for training initiatives for the voluntary sector via a scheme which is administered by the National Council for Voluntary Organisations; *Barclays Bank* has created a substantial fund to promote voluntary initiatives in the inner city; and the *Burton Group* has taken the lead in setting up a new schizophrenia charity called SANE (Schizophrenia A National Emergency), which is to be funded partly from high street charity shops selling manufacturers' ends-of-lines, and in promoting Design Works, a design centre in the North East being run in conjunction with the local enterprise agency, Project North-East. At a local level, *Community Links*, a social action project in the London Borough of Newham, has obtained sponsorship for its welfare advice project from a large local employer, *Tate & Lyle*, which can then tell its employees about this useful local service (and take credit for its support, notwithstanding the fact that the service is freely available to all local residents).

These are just some examples of companies beginning to allocate sizeable parts of their budget to charitable schemes with which they wish to be particularly closely identified. Such an association is intended to bring some benefit to the company, and the support given can extend beyond a simple transfer of cash – for example, Burton's support for Design Works comes largely in the form of a redundant warehouse (valued at £100,000), secondment of staff and professional help.

If charities were to begin to think in terms of sponsorship, to design schemes which would be attractive to and affordable by companies, and to make these requests known, then they might begin to tap this seam of company support. However, it is not quite as simple as this. Asking for sponsorship does not automatically mean that you will get more money; the company requires a respectable partner with a proven track record to collaborate with. The scheme also has to capture the interest of the company, and the benefits you are offering should be carefully considered and specified in your proposal. Even if you are a well-run organisation approaching the right company with an attractive scheme, there may still be problems. The company might misunderstand the request simply because it has come from a charity, and send you a small donation instead.

There is obviously a great deal of promotional work to be done on both sides. Companies need to understand the importance and benefits of sponsorship and how it can be used to their benefit. Charities, for their part, must recognise the essential difference between sponsorship and donations, and be aware of the very real opportunities that sponsorship offers for attracting funds. It is with these twin aims of promoting the opportunities of social sponsorship to companies and charities that a project called **Action Match** was established in 1989 by Community Links with Home Office support.

The benefits of sponsorship

Sponsorship is a loosely used term. It often means little more than a donation which is publicly acknowledged and which might therefore generate some good publicity for the donor. Applicants sometimes feel that if they suggest what they are looking for is 'sponsorship', they are more likely to be successful than if they were to request a donation; and companies may also think of their support as sponsorship because this sounds more impressive. But true sponsorship is more than a donation, it is a *partnership* between the donor and recipient.

In tax terms, a sponsorship would normally be classed as a business expense incurred 'wholly and exclusively' for the purpose of the business of the company, and it would also be subject to VAT as the provision of a service to the sponsor. In practical terms, it is also a business expense, with the company laying out its money in the expectation of some sort of return. That return may be *good publicity*, *media and press coverage*, or *PR* for the company or its brands, but there may also be other benefits – such as *entertainment* opportunities for staff generally as well as for senior directors, *access* to people such as TV personalities, royalty, politicians or other VIPs who may be already associated with or happy to do something for a good cause, opportunities for *involvement of employees* or retirees.

There may be something specific and valuable that you are able to offer a company. It is up to you to see the opportunities. What you can offer and the nature of the benefits it brings, will determine which budget (from within the company) will bear the cost and who will be responsible for deciding. Generally corporate publicity and other public relations benefits will be decided by the public affairs or corporate communications department at Head Office (different companies give this function different names) or occasionally by the donations manager. Anything that promotes a product or a brand will come out of a specific budget for that purpose. For example, *Coombes*, the bakers in Leicester, sponsored a Christmas production of 'Willie Wonka' at the local theatre, using money which would have otherwise been used in press advertising. The imaginative nature of the sponsorship which included special Wonka cakes on sale at the theatre, and window displays in bakery shops, produced far more public attention than a simple advertising campaign. A *Barratt*-sponsored fun-run was routed through a newly constructed Barratt Housing Estate, which the company was about to market, and the sponsorship money came from the marketing budget for that purpose.

The biggest budget of most companies is the budget for staff costs. It is here that particularly good opportunities may exist for attracting sponsorship, where the charity can provide welfare benefits, leisure opportunities, or some other service which will benefit company employees. For example, the amount a company spends on the staff Christmas party can dwarf what to you is a substantial sponsorship payment. So if you can provide real benefits, there is at least a basis to start thinking creatively.

There may be other special reasons why a company might want to undertake a sponsorship, for example:

● To celebrate an anniversary such as a centenary by sponsoring something special.

● To overcome a particular PR problem – they may be seen as noisy, dirty, smelly or be trying to improve their image locally as part of an effort to secure planning or other approval for something they wish to do.

● To coincide with a product launch, or the opening of a branch or factory or the award of a major contract at home or overseas.

● To be identified with the qualities your organisation represents (such as innovation or community concern) as part of a wider PR strategy.

● To link with brand advertising (such as the *Mars* London Marathon).

● To provide training or experience for staff or trainees such as participating in a conservation volunteer scheme).

How companies decide

Because of the closer involvement and also because of the larger sums of money involved, a company will adopt very different criteria in deciding which sponsorship proposals to proceed with than for its charitable donations programme. It will be looking at its own needs and for the proposal that matches these needs, but it also needs to be sure that the organisation it is sponsoring has objects at least compatible with its own, and that there is the professional expertise there to carry out the sponsorship as set out in the proposal.

The difference between sponsorship and donations is well illustrated by the different guidelines adopted by a large company in assessing sponsorship proposals and grant applications. The guidelines here are those used by *Shell UK*; the annotations are our own.

1. Sponsorship criteria *(used by Shell)*

Appropriateness
Is the activity/event appropriate to the sponsor (having regard to the nature of the sponsor's business and the work of the organisation seeking sponsorship)?

Partnership
Is there scope for partnership, or is the applicant simply seeking money?

Real involvement
What involvement is being looked for from the sponsor, and how well does this meet the needs of the sponsor?

Continuity
Is there scope for a continuing relationship (over the next few years), or is the activity/event just a one-off?

Initiative

Does the sponsorship represent a new initiative, something that would not happen without the company's support? Is it interesting and lively? It is much more attractive to back an interesting proposal and an interesting organisation.

'Professional' approach

Has the applicant approached the business of getting sponsorship in a professional way, and can he demonstrate a similar professionalism in the running of his organisation?

Visibility

How 'visible' will the event be, and what specific publicity and PR benefits will accrue to the sponsor?

Value for money

Does the deal represent value for money? What are the benefits and how much money is being asked from the sponsor? How does this rate as compared with other possible sponsorships that the company might consider? The relationship of cost to return and the importance of the return to the company is the dominant factor affecting the decision to sponsor or not to sponsor.

2. Grant guidelines *(used by Shell)*

National organisations

Grants from *head office* are made to national organisations, and not to local branches or affiliates of national organisations or to purely local organisations.

Non-political

Charitable grants are not made for political purposes or to organisations which are deemed to be too 'political'.

Not 'bricks and mortar'

'Bricks and mortar' building appeals are not supported; the company prefers to give its money for people and activities (whilst other companies may and some do support bricks and mortar appeals).

Close to major company locations

Local charities active close to the company's major employment centres are supported. Such charities benefit employees, their families and the local community generally, and their support can provide good local publicity. Normally local grant decisions will involve the local management. Applications may be dealt with locally at the discretion of the local manager/director or be processed centrally.

Employee involvement

The involvement of the company's employees with the applicant organisation is a very significant factor for deciding who the company should support. Employees can be involved in an official capacity (as trustees), or as volunteers, or in helping raise money for the charity. Wherever there is some employee involvement, this should be mentioned in the application.

Pilot initiatives of potential national significance
The support of a pilot project (which works) will bring credit to the company, and will be seen as particularly cost-effective in view of the further developments arising from its success. Traditionally grant-making trusts have favoured innovation whilst companies have tended to play safe. However some of the larger and more thoughtful company givers are now happy to promote innovation.

Business links
Educational projects which link schools to business are a current priority concern for many companies, particularly those concerned with science and technology.

Good chance project will develop concerted efforts
Where the donation of money can encourage the recipient to encourage and draw upon the voluntary efforts of its supporters, this makes the appeal a more attractive prospect for the donor.

This is just one company's list of guidelines. Some factors not included here, which are important to many companies, are: (a) support for enterprise, employment and training projects, which increasingly large companies are giving priority to; and (b) leverage, where a smallish donation can be used to have a more substantial effect. Leverage can be defined in many different ways, but if there is a leverage factor then it does no harm to stress it. Every company knows that the individual grants or donations it makes are relatively quite small in size, but likes to feel that the money is being well spent and effectively spent.

Listing the benefits

Generally speaking, as part of the sponsorship proposal, the applicant will list the actual tangible benefits which it hopes will accrue to the company. It is as well to list benefits in two categories – those benefits which will require an input of resources by the charity, and those which the charity can provide at no extra cost to itself. Having made such a list, it is worth thinking a little harder to find additional benefits which could be provided which might make the proposal more attractive.

Here is a list of benefits offered by the National Theatre for the sponsorship of its after-work 'PLATFORM Performances'. This was sponsored in the mid-1980s by *Network South East*. Waterloo Station is a stone's throw away (note the geographical link and the platform connection), and Network South East was promoting Capital Card with a range of ticket-holder special offers – which included reduced price tickets for NT PLATFORM Performances as part of the sponsorship deal. So the NT ended up not just with money, but with a promotion to a potentially new audience.

There are approximately 150 PLATFORM Performances each year and a total audience of 20,000 rising to 25,000 people. The cost of presenting National Theatre PLATFORMS is £30,000 for one year and in return the NT was offering the sponsor the following benefits:

1. The sponsor's name and value of sponsorship (if desired) to be credited in all NT press releases issued on the securing of sponsorship for NT PLATFORMS.

2. A prominent programme acknowledgement to the sponsor in Olivier and Lyttelton Theatre programmes.

3. The sponsor's name/logo to be credited on all single sheet PLATFORM programmes which have a print run of 20,000 per annum.

4. Approximately 10,000 special programmes are designed for celebrity PLATFORMS and the sponsor's name/logo would be acknowledged on these.

5. The NT produces a repertoire leaflet 8 times or more a year which has a total print run of 100,000 per printing. PLATFORMS are listed in the calendar Mondays to Saturdays, and are also detailed in a special column in this leaflet. The sponsor of NT PLATFORMS would receive an appropriate credit in the repertoire leaflet.

6. The NT was introducing an eye-catching poster advertising PLATFORMS. Posters would be displayed in the NT's foyers and the sponsor's name/logo would be acknowledged.

7. The sponsor's name/logo would appear on the PLATFORMS leaflets which advertise the programmes in advance. These are distributed with every PLATFORM ticket sold and are displayed in the NT's foyers.

8. A number of complimentary tickets to Olivier and Lyttelton Theatre productions to be made available to the sponsor during the period of the sponsorship (amount to be agreed by NT).

9. A number of complimentary tickets to PLATFORMS to be made available to the sponsor during the period of the sponsorship (amount to be agreed by NT).

10. Special arrangements can be made for the sponsor to entertain their guests at the National Theatre. The NT has magnificent foyers, with splendid bars and buffets; there is also a restaurant with banqueting facilities for over 100.

11. A credit thanking the sponsor and promoting NT PLATFORMS would appear on the National Theatre's illuminated electronic Sefact sign measuring 40' × 8' which overlooks the Thames and Waterloo Bridge – the busiest pedestrian bridge in London – five days a week including Saturday nights and Sundays. The value of the sponsorship could be shown if the sponsor wished. (Timing and amount of exposure to be agreed between the sponsor and the NT).

Ideas for sponsorship

Each year the Association for Business Sponsorship of the Arts awards prizes for the best sponsorship. The citations list provides a snapshot of current trends and ideas for good sponsorship, particularly for smaller sponsorships by first-time sponsors and for the sponsorship of special interests. In 1988, prizes were awarded for the following sponsorships:

Gordon Richards Tools, who only employ 18 people, celebrated their twentieth anniversary by sponsoring a City of Birmingham Symphony Orchestra concert. The occasion was used to entertain customers, and an exhibition was mounted to coincide with the concert. This sponsorship showed how a small company could successfully dovetail business and arts objectives in a sponsorship package.

The sponsorship of *Jamdani Restaurants* made it possible for the Whitechapel Art Gallery to present 'Woven Air' – an exhibition of the muslin and Kantha embroidery tradition of Bangladesh. The exhibition also forged strong links between a major contemporary art gallery and the large Bangladeshi community which lives in the area.

Volkswagen (VAG United Kingdom) sponsored the launch which established the Tate Gallery in Liverpool. The sponsorship of the project included a highly original advertising campaign and a publicity van with an exterior designed by David Hockney.

Beck's Bier (marketed in the UK by Scottish & Newcastle Breweries) is primarily targeted at style-conscious 18–45 year olds. To enhance its image with this group, the company used sponsorship as part of its marketing strategy, supporting innovative and alternative art forms such as the Red Shift Theatre Company, Dance Umbrella and the Théatre de Complicité's national tour. Their large-scale and continuing corporate sponsorship programme set new standards and demonstrated that sponsors do not always have to play safe.

The Council for Music in Hospitals has been bringing live music to hospitals for 40 years, but visiting hospices is a new venture for them, made possible by the sponsorship of *Napp Laboratories*. The programme brought enormous pleasure to the patients. This sensitive sponsorship reinforced Napp's corporate commitment to improving the quality of life.

Further information

For information on the **Action Match** service, contact David Robinson at Community Links, 81 High Street South, London E8 4EJ (01-472 6652), or Mandy Wilson at Action Match, 14–18 West Bar Green, Sheffield S1 2DA (0742-723651).

For information on the **Association for Business Sponsorship** of the Arts, contact ABSA, 2 Chester Street, London SW1X 7BB (01-235 9781). ABSA publishes the *Business and Arts Bulletin*, this together with the ABSA annual report, which lists all ABSA member companies and details of the sponsorship activities of many of them, is available on subscription. ABSA also publishes *The Sponsor's Guide*. This covers the uses of sponsorship, setting a policy, making a choice, selecting activities, exploiting extra opportunities, achieving objectives working with an arts organisation, budgeting, getting value for money, tax and VAT, the *Business Sponsorship Incentive Scheme*, sample contracts and letters of agreement. Although aimed principally at sponsors, the publication will also be of interest to those seeking sponsorship.

Helpful organisations for the sponsorship of environmental projects are the **World Wide Fund for Nature**, 11–13 Ockford Road, Godalming, Surrey GU7 1QU (0486-820551), **UK 2000**, Unit 101, Butlers Wharf Business Centre, 45 Curlew Street, London SE1 2ND (01-370 1047), and the **Groundwork Foundation**, Bennett's Court, Bennett's Hull, Birmingham B2 5ST (021-236 8565).

Gifts in Kind

Faced with an avalanche of appeals from charities for cash support, many companies find that they are able to meet only a small fraction of these appeals. They are unable or unwilling to expand their donations budgets, so it makes sense to start thinking of other ways in which they can give support.

One way is to give 'in kind'. This can make a great deal of sense. The support that is given can be given at little or no real cost to the company, yet it can be worth a great deal to the recipient charity. Where the company is giving its products, it is in a sense a self-advertisement for these products, and if the company has developed a formal policy for its in-kind giving, these gifts can be directed into areas where the company wishes to make a real impact. Computer companies, such as *IBM*, *Digital*, and *Hewlett Packard*, all have policies linking their support in kind to supporting education at various levels.

A company has much more to give than its products. It can give raw materials or scrap or offcuts. It can give damaged stock or ends of lines of items which are no longer in the current range. It can give trade-ins (in 1988, *Amstrad* offered a large discount on its word processors to anyone trading in a typewriter, and then offered these typewriters free through its dealer network to any charity). It can offer facilities such as meeting rooms (in 1989 *BP* hosted a charity reception organised by the Charity Commission, and *IBM* a strategy discussion on directions for Save the Children in the 1990s), places on training courses, printing of leaflets, design. Where the company is a professional promotion consultant, it can take on charity clients, for small jobs at least, on a free basis. (*Saatchi and Saatchi*, besides their formal procedure for this, also run seminars on public relations for charities). Accountants can be asked to be honorary auditors, and solicitors honorary legal advisers.

A further aspect of support in kind is in the form of staff time. A separate chapter has been devoted to secondment and other forms of staff help.

Often it is far easier to obtain support in kind than a cash donation. Although there is no precise information on the level of in-kind support that companies give to charity, we believe that it is likely to be very substantial.

To get in-kind support, you have to ask a company which has the item or facilities you require. Anyone might give you a cash donation, but only an estate agent or surveyor can give you a free building survey, only a builder's merchant or building materials company or garden centre can give you paving stones, and so on. Because there is this added connection, it makes it easier for you to ask. And when you do ask they will realise why you are approaching them – which makes it more difficult for them to refuse.

Your most successful approach for soliciting gifts in kind is likely to be by telephone. This will be much harder to refuse. Try to identify the person who is able to make the decision and ring them up. If that sounds too easy, it's because it is easy – although it does require a certain amount of nerve and a good telephone presence.

A variety of people might be able to say yes: the managing director, the general manager, the warehouseman. . . . The best way of asking is to explain that you are a charity, that your cause is important and why you need what you are asking for: 'I'm from Anytown Age Concern. We are a local charity and part of a national network of local Age Concerns. We provide a whole range of facilities for the elderly. We are just refurnishing our day centre in High Street which is used by over 50 elderly people a day. We need a 25 inch colour TV. I wonder if you would like to donate an ex-rental set in good working order. . . .' It will soon be obvious whether the company is interested or not. If it is interested, then use all your persuasive skills. Make it easy for them to say yes. . . . 'One of our volunteer drivers can collect it whenever it is convenient' . . . or 'A feature on the new centre will appear in the local paper and they've agreed to mention the names of companies that have given support' . . . or 'Tele-rent, down the road have agreed to donate one of the two sets we need.'

If you can't get a donation, try to get something out of the call. Suggest that perhaps in some corner there is an old model which they are not going to sell, which you will put to good use, or that they might be able to offer you a substantial discount. Some charities have achieved discounts of up to 50%, which may not in fact cost the company anything since it may well be selling via a commercial distributor at a hefty discount.

Remember to ask for a discount on all your purchases (if you cannot get the item donated). This shows a cost conscious charity, and it also makes it easier to raise money. If you can show that you are getting a 50% discount, then a cash donation of the remaining 50% of the price will go twice as far. This 'leverage' which increases the value of the donation to the recipient makes it more attractive for the donor.

The start for gifts in kind is to make a 'shopping list' of the items you require. Include services as well as 'things' – for example two hours of a book-keeper's time once a month. Then try to put the name and the telephone number of potential donors to each item. A local business phone directory or a trade directory of some sort is an ideal starting point.

As an actual example, here is a shopping list made by a countryside conservation project.

A garage base	Overhead projector
Free servicing of a Land Rover	Computer
Loan of a Sherpa Personnel carrier for 3 months	Typewriter
Fuel	Trees and plants
Technical and management service	Fencing and gate materials
Photocopying	Construction materials
Office accommodation	Tools
Office furniture	Chain saws

The total value of gifts achieved by this charity amounted to £36,800 in 50 separate donations, with labour and running costs for the work paid for by the Community Programme. Donors included the County Council, other charities such as a County Nature Conservation Trust and the National Trust, local farms, large and small companies, and a number of individuals. This example shows the potential for soliciting support in kind. Although it will inevitably involve a great deal of hard work to get support in this way, it may be much harder, chancier or even impossible to raise this level of support in the form of cash donations.

If you are successful you are not only raising support, but you will be opening up supply lines for the future. If you treat your donors well, it will be much easier to go back next time you need something. So treat an in-kind donor in exactly the same way as you treat a cash donor:

● Say thank you.

● Report back at the end of the project.

● Acknowledge the support, and its value, in your Annual Report.

● Get publicity for the donation where you can and when you feel it appropriate.

● Put the supporter on your 'donor list' to receive regular information about your work.

● Invite them to 'open days' and other events.

● Do everything you can to make them feel that their support really has benefited you and helped you in your work.

Tax-effective company giving

It is obviously advantageous if company support is given tax-effectively. Either this will increase the value of the donation in the hands of the charity at no additional cost to the company, or it will reduce the cost to the company of making the donation. Either way, less tax is paid, which is in effect a contribution from the Exchequer.

Any charity thinking of approaching companies is well advised to understand the different ways in which companies can give their support tax-effectively. Particularly for smaller companies who may not be aware of the tax situation, you may be able to help them by suggesting tax-effective ways of making their gift. The larger companies will normally know the ground rules and have organised their giving accordingly.

In this chapter we try to explain the different methods of tax-effective giving.

The mechanics of tax-effective company giving

When an individual makes a donation, he/she pays a sum out of after-tax income and you (the charity) are subsequently able to reclaim Basic Rate Income Tax from the Inland Revenue where the donation has been made by Deed of Covenant.

When a company makes a cash donation, the procedure is somewhat different. A company is subject to Corporation Tax on its earnings. Paying a donation (using a tax-effective method) means that the cost of the donation can be deducted from the company's income before Corporation Tax is charged. This reduces the amount of the company's taxable profits on which tax is levied. If donations are paid in a way which is not tax-effective, the donation has to be paid out of the company's after-tax income.

In order to achieve this saving, the donation has to be paid in one of two ways:

1. Donation: The donation has to be made as an annual payment under a Deed of Covenant or, in certain circumstances, as a single payment, from which Income Tax at the basic rate (25% in 1988–89) has been deducted. This Income Tax that has been deducted from the amount of the donation has to be accounted for to the Inland Revenue and will be subsequently reclaimed by the charity.

For every £100 which the company gives, it will have to deduct £25 in Income Tax (which is paid to the Inland Revenue), and pay the charity £75. Expressed the other way round, for every £100 the company pays directly to the charity, it has to pay £33.33 in Income Tax to the Inland Revenue (which the charity reclaims), so that the charity receives a total of £133.33.

2. Business expenditure: The support has to be given in a way that it can be considered an item of business expenditure (e.g. sponsorship or advertising) which is accepted by the Inland Revenue as expenditure having been made by the company wholly and exclusively for the purposes of its trade.

Ways of giving tax-effectively

The two ways in which companies can make donations from which Income Tax has been deducted are:

1. Covenant payments: All companies can make charitable donations by Deed of Covenant, but the company has to commit itself to giving its support for 4 years (or longer).

2. Single payments: In 1986, the Finance Act introduced a new procedure where single payments could be made to charity and be tax-deductible. Certain conditions need to be met:

(a) The company making the payment should not be a Close Company. A Close Company is a company under the control of a limited number of individuals. Broadly, where a company is controlled by more than 5 persons (including family interests) or has 25% or more of shares publicly quoted on a recognised Stock Exchange, it will not be a Close Company.

(b) Income Tax should be deducted when the donation is made and paid to the Inland Revenue. The company supplies the charity with a Certificate of Deduction of Tax, and the charity reclaims the Income Tax that has been deducted from the Inland Revenue (as for covenant payments).

(c) The total payments made using this procedure should in any one accounting period not exceed 3% of the gross dividends paid by the company to its ordinary shareholders for the same accounting period.

Whether the company decides to make a single payment (as above) or a covenanted donation, it can choose to pay the donation to:

(a) The charity directly. This means that the charity is responsible for reclaiming the Income Tax.

(b) A company trust or a half-way house charity (such as the Charities Aid Foundation) which acts as intermediary for the donation, receiving the net donation, reclaiming the Income Tax, and paying a gross sum to the charity. In such circumstances the charity simply receives a sum of money as a one-off payment in exactly the same way as it receives donations from a grant-making trust. It is not responsible for reclaiming Income Tax, which has already been done. Any 4-year commitment by the company is with the intermediary charity or company trust and not with the beneficiary charity.

The tax benefits for a company

The mathematics of tax-effective company giving are quite complicated to explain. The following factors have to be considered:

Companies pay Corporation Tax at four different rates, depending on the level of profit they are earning.

Income Tax, not Corporation Tax, has to be deducted at the Basic Rate from the donation.

The donation can be stated as a net or a gross sum. Net Deeds and Gross Deeds are explained in the next paragraph. The amount paid immediately by the charity is the net donation. The cost to the company is the gross donation, which is the amount paid to the charity plus the Income Tax paid to the Inland Revenue, which is subsequently reclaimed by the charity.

The actual cost to the company is the after-tax cost of the donation. Because any item of expenditure reduces the company's profits, this means that there will be a tax saving (the amount depending on the company's tax rate) if the donation is made tax-effectively. The after-tax cost to a company of giving £100 in various ways is as follows (all tax rates for 1988–89):

1. If a company simply makes a £100 donation which is not tax-effective, for example by writing out a cheque for this amount, the after-tax cost will be £100.

2. If a company makes a gross donation of £100 under covenant (by using a Gross Deed) or using the Single Payment Procedure, it has to pay £75 as a net payment to the charity and £25 as the Income Tax to the Inland Revenue. The charity receives a total of £100. The after tax cost of this will be:

Company tax rate	After tax cost to a company of £100 gross donation	Tax benefit
Nil	£100.00	Nil
25%	£75.00	£25.00
35%	£65.00	£35.00
37.5%	£62.50	£37.50

If the company decides to pass on the whole of this tax benefit to charity by increasing its donation, the table below shows the amount it could give at an after-tax cost of £100 (which is the same cost as making a £100 donation not tax-effectively):

Company tax rate	Gross donation at after-tax cost of £100	Net payment to the charity
Nil	£100.00	£75.00
25%	£133.33	£100.00
35%	£153.85	£115.38
37.5%	£160.00	£120.00

These figures show the extent of the tax benefits of company giving.

3. If a company gives £100 to the charity as a net payment under covenant (by using a Net Deed) or using the Single Payment Procedure, then the gross cost of the payment is £133.33 (£100 to the charity and £33.33 to the Inland Revenue in Income Tax). The charity receives a total of £133.33. The after-tax cost of this donation will be:

Company tax rate	After-tax cost to a company of £100 net donation
Nil	£133.33
25%	£100.00
35%	£86.67
37.5%	£83.33

Note that where a company pays Corporation Tax, it is never more expensive and may be substantially cheaper for a company to give £100 net than to give £100 not tax-effectively.

Net and Gross Deeds

1. A Gross Deed describes the payment to the charity as '£... less Income Tax at the basic rate'. The amount stated in the Deed is the amount paid directly to the charity AND the amount of Income Tax deducted which is paid to the Inland Revenue and reclaimed by the charity. The total cost of the donation to the company is the amount stated in the Deed, and this is also the value of the donation to the charity.

2. A Net Deed describes the donation as 'a sum of money which after deduction of Income Tax at the basic rate will amount to £...'. The amount stated in the Deed is the amount paid to the charity. This is a payment net of Income Tax at the basic rate (25% in 1988–89). Income Tax has to be paid at the rate of £33.33 for every £100 paid to the charity. This Income Tax is paid to the Inland Revenue and subsequently recovered by the charity. The total cost of the donation is £133.33 (Income Tax at 25% on this sum = £33.33), and this is also the value of the donation to the charity.

If a company decides to make a donation to a charity, it can use either a Gross Deed or a Net Deed. If it uses a Net Deed, it will cost the company one third more than the amount stated in the Deed. But if the company pays UK Corporation Tax, the after-tax cost of the donation will be either the same as or less than the amount stated in the Deed.

Normally companies prefer to use a Gross Deed. The cost of the donation to the company is the total of the two payments the . company has to make (to the charity and to the Inland Revenue).

If a charity asks a company to give £100 by Deed of Covenant and supplies a Net Deed, it will cost the company one third more than where a Gross Deed is used, but the charity will also receive one third more. Most companies may not notice this difference, which is, in any case, never more than the tax saving.

Net and Gross Single Payments

If a charity receives a single payment from a company that is not a Close Company, then either:

1. The payment has been made as a net payment after deduction of Income Tax (Single Payment Procedure). The company has deducted Income Tax and will supply the charity with a Certificate of Deduction of Tax (either with the payment or in due course), and will account to the Inland Revenue for the tax deducted within 14 days of the end of the quarter in which the payment was made (by 14 April, 14 July, 14 October, 14 January following the date of the payment).

2. The company was unaware of the Single Payment Procedure and has made a donation which will have to be paid out of its after-tax income.

Legislation for the Single Payment Procedure clearly states that tax has to be deducted from the donation 'at the time the donation is made'. Since the tax does not have to be accounted for until after the end of the quarter, the position can be rectified retrospectively.

If you receive a single payment from a company that is not a

Close Company and which is not a payment made by a company charitable trust, then you can remind the company of the benefits of using the Single Payment Procedure and enclose a Certificate of Deduction of Tax (forms obtainable from the Inland Revenue) with the amount and date of the donation already filled in for the company to sign and return. The donation you have already received is the net amount, and tax has to be paid by the company at the rate of £33.33 for every £100 given. By doing this, not only will you be able to increase the value of the donation by one third, but the company may also be able to save on the cost of the donation. You need to check that the company is not a Close Company before suggesting this. Most privately owned companies are Close Companies; most publicly quoted companies are not Close Companies.

Deposited covenants

It is possible for a company to enter into a Deposited Covenant agreement in just the same way as for an individual donor. The company advances all four covenant payments at the outset under a separate loan agreement.

Most non-Close companies would probably prefer to pay the donation all at once using the Single Payment Procedure (already described), rather than the more complicated Deposited Covenant procedure.

Giving via Company Trusts

Many larger companies have established a Company Trust as their vehicle for tax-effective giving. The company makes donations to the trust (by covenant or single payment) which reclaims Income Tax and distributes the money (gross) to the charities the company wishes to benefit at the company's direction.

Sometimes the trust also has its own capital resources which are invested to yield an income; and that income is distributed in addition to any income transferred by the company.

Charities Aid Foundation Service

CAF offers a tailor-made service to companies which combines tax-effective giving, flexibility in choice of charity, and ease of administration.

The company pays the whole of its donations budget as one annual covenant payment (normally a 4-year covenant for a fixed annual sum or a percentage of the company's annual pre-tax profits) or using the Single Payment Procedure (not available to Close Companies). Tax is deducted from the total the company wishes to give and accounted for to the Inland Revenue. The company issues a Certificate of Deduction of Tax to CAF, and CAF reclaims the Income Tax from the Inland Revenue in the normal way.

The total given (including reclaimed tax) is held to the company's account, and the company issues instructions, either in writing to CAF or using 'vouchers' which are sent to the charity, and payments are then made from this account to the charities chosen by the company.

Using this procedure, only one tax payment need be accounted for each year and one Certificate of Deduction of Tax issued by the company. The beneficiary charities receive a gross sum and do not have to go to the bother of reclaiming tax. The company is not committed to supporting a particular charity more than once, although there is a commitment to continue payments to the company's CAF account according to the terms of the covenant.

No charge is made for this service, but the company has to make a compulsory donation to the National Council for Voluntary Organisations, the national charity which established the service. This amounts to 3% of the sum available for distribution for sums up to £10,000, 1% thereafter, with a maximum of £550 on sums of £35,000 or more. Full details of the service are available from the Charities Aid Foundation, 48 Pembury Road, Tonbridge, Kent TN9 2JD.

Sponsorship

Sponsorship is a term which is quite loosely used by companies as well as by charities. For tax purposes, sponsorship must be able to be considered a proper business expense, that is an expenditure which is incurred wholly and exclusively for the purposes of the company's trade. This means that the benefits to the company should be reasonable in relation to the cost of the sponsorship. These benefits will be spelled out by you in your sponsorship application.

There are a number of points to note:

1. Not all sponsorship is incurred 'wholly and exclusively' for trade purposes. If the Inland Revenue consider the expenditure unreasonably high in relation to the benefits, then they will disallow the whole amount when assessing the company's Corporation Tax liability. Since the money has not been paid over as a donation, it will be disallowed on that count too. Much will depend on the attitude of the local tax inspector. But the problems of 'dual purpose' sponsorship can be overcome by splitting the support into two parts, a donation (paid tax-effectively) and a sponsorship payment (a business expense). For non-Close companies, it is sufficient that the 'sponsorship' payment be made under deduction of tax using the Single Payment Procedure described earlier. It is not possible (at least in theory) to pay for sponsorship by Deed of Covenant or out of funds provided via an intermediary trust, as such funds should not be used for payments which confer an appreciable benefit on the company.

2. Sponsorship of capital is not an allowable expense. If a building is 'sponsored', the money should be paid as a donation.

3. Entertainment is not normally an allowable business expense. Sponsorship often includes some form of entertainment facilities. The best way of dealing with the entertainment element of a sponsorship is for the cost of providing these facilities to be separated out and invoiced for separately (plus VAT if the charity is registered for VAT).

4. Sponsorship can produce a VAT liability. It is considered the provision of a business service by the charity to company. If the charity is registered for VAT (or if it would be obliged to register as a result of the sponsorship income), then the charity will invoice the company for the amount of the sponsorship plus the VAT thereon. If the company is itself registered for VAT, it will be able to offset the VAT it has to pay against its VAT liability on its

own sales. The VAT situation should be discussed when the sponsorship is being negotiated.

Advertising

Advertising in charity publications (such as annual reports, event programmes, magazines and newsletters, brochures, etc.) has been a common method of supporting charity.

Such advertising will normally be considered a business expense. The advertiser will keep a 'voucher copy' of the advertisement as evidence of its business purpose. As a business expense, it will be allowable for tax. There are a number of advantages of 'donations' given in the form of advertising:

The support is given as a single payment made directly to a charity, without deduction of tax, signed Deeds of Covenant or other complications.

It is a particularly attractive method of support for smaller companies which have not sorted out a procedure for charitable giving.

However, there are a number of reasons why a donation might be preferable:

1. Advertising always incurs a cost in printing the advertisement, so less of the money goes to support charitable work.

2. VAT will be chargeable (if the charity is registered for VAT) except where two conditions are met: the advertisements are clearly not of a commercial character and the publication includes a significant proportion of non-business advertisements from private individuals; in such cases, Customs and Excise will treat the advertisement payment as a donation.

3. A third problem of brochure advertising is the disrepute that has been brought by commercial agencies acting on a commission basis or passing on only small amounts of the advertising receipts to the charity; in such cases the payment which is intended for charity goes largely to support the printer and the agent. It is up to the trustees of the charity to guard against malpractice and to ensure that a reasonable part of the payment for the advertisement, which the donor considers to be a charitable payment, goes to support the work of the charity.

In kind support

Companies can and do give substantially in kind. The tax implications of in-kind support divide into two categories.

1. Gifts that do not need to be accounted for

Gifts of facilities, waste, items or equipment about to be discarded, and the occasional gift of value would not normally be accounted for. These can simply be given away.

2. Gifts that have to be accounted for

Gifts of some value (either substantial gifts or smaller gifts made frequently) cannot be simply 'lost' as stock shrinkage. The options open to a company are:

(a) To write the value of the item down to zero in the company's books, in which case no VAT is payable. Wherever possible, this is the best procedure to adopt.

(b) To sell the item to the charity, or to a company trust which then donates it to the charity. The company would donate the cost of purchase to the trust as a tax-effective cash donation. The selling price would normally be the book value of the item plus VAT, which would be payable on the sale.

(c) To lend the item to the charity.

In occasional circumstances, the gift could be considered a gift in furtherance of the trade of the company and there is a special provision which makes the cost of such gifts an allowable business expense (Section 577 of the Taxes Act, and Extra Statutory Concession B7 if the gift is made to a local body).

If the item is simply given, the company might find that the cost of the gift is disallowed as a business expense in calculating its Corporation Tax liability and that VAT is charged on the book value of the gift.

PART II

THE
APPROACH

How to do an appeal

What companies can give you

Many charities are completely unrealistic about what they might obtain from companies. The business of companies is business, and charitable giving is only ever a sideline. Even for the bigger companies, the sums that are given to individual charities are quite modest, and they seldom make long-term commitments.

A generous donation from a very large company might be only £1,000 and rarely more than £2,500. Smaller companies give proportionately less, and local branch outlets might be unable to give more than £25. Obviously there are exceptions, where the appeal is particularly relevant or appropriate to the company.

It pays to be clear about how much you are likely to receive or what else you might ask for *before you make your approach*. As we have seen, there is a great deal more that companies can give than just cash, and often this non-cash support can be much more valuable than a cash donation. The *Allied Dunbar* case study at the end of the book shows how a leading company makes its resources available to local community organisations.

The following are some of the other things you might wish to ask companies to give you:

● **Advertising in brochures** or newsletters. Many smaller companies often are prepared to give in this way, if asked. This can be treated as a business expense, so that there are no tax complications. Remember though that advertising support is never as valuable to you as a cash donation, as you will have to pay the costs of printing the publication containing the advertisements.

● **Sponsoring your annual report.** You have to produce an annual report. This provides you with a good opportunity to raise money and acknowledge the support. Some large companies may even be able to print the report in-house. Sponsorship of an annual report is a particularly good idea if you are producing a rather more lavish report than usual, which you can then use to promote your organisation and develop its fund-raising. Acknowledging the support will also highlight the fact that you are actually doing something to raise money, which can help you with your other fund-raising. One problem is that your annual report will have a life span of only one year. It may be better to produce a review of your charity's work and to insert a more cheaply produced financial report inside this.

● **Sponsoring an event** or activity either locally or nationally. This can range from a bona fide sponsorship, when what the sponsor gets out of the arrangement is crucial, to what is really little more than a publicised donation. Some sponsorship comes out of charitable budgets, some out of corporate PR budgets, and some out of the marketing or advertising budgets for particular products or brands. In each case the decision structure may be different.

● **Gifts in kind.** A company can provide the goods or services it produces, materials, redundant equipment or furniture often at little cost to itself, and this can be of immense value to a charity. Contact those individual companies who might help. For smaller companies, use the telephone and go straight to the top. Another approach is to write a 'shopping list' of items you require – anything from a set of law books for a legal advice centre, to furnishings for a day centre or your office, and to circulate this with a covering letter to likely companies. Many 'high street' companies will also be happy to provide raffle prizes if you contact the local store manager.

● **Advice and help.** Anything from a full-time secondment to helping on a specific task either in or out of office hours. If there is something you particularly need that you think a company can give you, then it is worth asking. This can be an extremely cost-effective way for a company to give support.

● **Other services.** Companies have been known to donate all kinds of services, from printing leaflets, allowing you to use the photocopier, putting your post through their franking machine, making places available on training courses, lending a room for a reception, and so on. Again this can be done at little or no cost to the company.

● **Contacts.** The support of senior company people can be very helpful in fund-raising from the business community. It can also on occasion be helpful in your dealings with your local authority and in bringing a more businesslike approach to the planning of what you are doing. Some charities have found it extremely beneficial to have senior business people as Committee Members or Trustees.

● **Employee support.** Some companies undertake fund-raising drives for particular charities. A good example is *John Laing*, where staff raised £370,000 for the NSPCC Centenary in 1984 which was matched by £250,000 of company support, and in 1988 a similar drive was organised for Great Ormond Street and other children's hospitals. Another aspect of employee support is payroll giving which is likely to become a more prominent feature of charitable giving in future years.

Who to contact

Personal contact if you already have it, or if you can develop it, is extremely important. This has traditionally been the best means of approach. Today, even where the company has a well-defined donations policy, a personal approach to the Chairman, Managing Director, or some senior director will not harm your chances. And this applies both for a national charity approaching large national companies, as well as local charities approaching firms in their particular local area. One large national charity claims that it only ever approaches companies through personal contact; and where it has not got or cannot find any point of contact it does not even bother sending a written appeal. This is obviously extreme, and many charities can and do run successful postal appeals.

So if you are planning an appeal, it is obviously an important first step to find which of your committee members, your trustees, your patrons and your vice-presidents (or whatever device you have for getting the great and good associated with your particular charity) have influence, or know people who have. If you can find someone who knows the chairman or a board member on the main board of the company and ask them to write a personal letter, then this will prove useful. It will also be helpful if you can discover some of the particular interests of one or other of the directors. If you are working in the field of the physically or mentally handicapped, for example, it may be that one of the directors of the company you are approaching has had a handicapped child and would therefore be prone to support your cause.

But if you haven't got a contact and can see no way of developing one, then you will have to make do without. You will need to discover the person in the company responsible for handling charity appeals. For smaller companies it will be the Chairman or Managing Director. Larger companies will probably have somebody usually at a quite senior level who is responsible for handling the company's donations. These people are usually based at the company HQ, and their titles vary from company to company; some are located within the Company Secretary's department, some in the finance department, some in the personnel department, some are the personal assistant to the General Manager or Managing Director. Some companies will make the actual decisions in consultation with the Chairman, some have at a special Appeals Committee, whilst for others it may come up at a main Board Meeting. If you can try to find out who to write to and then address the letter personally to that person, it will improve your chances of success. Paradoxically, the smaller the company, the more important it will be to make a personal approach.

If you are sending a written appeal, it is important to try to get someone who is a 'name' to sign your appeal letter. If you have a prominent supporter who is known in your own field of good works, then it would be helpful to try to associate this person with your appeal. People will feel that if so-and-so is closely involved, then your charity must be worth supporting. This is a means of building a bridge between the two very different worlds of industry and charity, by obtaining an endorsement from someone whose opinion is respected.

Developing points of personal contact and gleaning as much information as you can about the companies you feel you should be approaching is something you have to build up over the years. Keep a card index, update it each year and use it to record any significant bits of information that will help you in your future fund-raising.

Which companies to approach

Rather than send out a circular mailing to 100 or 1,000 companies, you will be more successful if you select those companies that you believe will be particularly interested in your project. In the past, many charities have sent out circular appeals. But today such is the competition for funds, that most charities are well advised to send their appeals to those companies where they feel they stand a reasonable chance of getting support.

Where you have identified a company that you think might be particularly interested in your work, then it is worth approaching that company specifically with an individually written appeal. Where you can, try to find a good reason why you believe the company should support you and include this prominently in your letter.

The companies to approach must depend on what sort of organisation you are. If you are a national organisation, then an appeal to the country's leading companies is appropriate. Local groups should approach local firms and local branches of national companies which have a presence in their area of operation. All organisations can approach companies in connected fields; for example, a housing project can appeal to building companies, property developers, estate agents etc.

There may be occasions where a charity will not want to accept money from a company in a related industry – a health education charity may not want to accept money from a tobacco or brewery company or from the confectionery industry, as it might feel that as a result of doing so it would be seen to be compromised. Each charity has to judge where it draws the line.

You will find the names and addresses of companies, some-times with the names of the Managing Director and other details in a whole series of useful directories. The top 1,300 corporate donors are listed in **A Guide to Company Giving**. The top 350 donors are covered in greater detail in the companion **Major Companies Guide**.

The top 1,000 companies in the UK, together with the leading companies in other sectors and overseas, are listed in the **Times 1,000**. The **Kompass Register of British Industry and Commerce** lists members of the CBI and is available in regional sections. The **Guide to Key British Enterprises** is a huge directory of leading firms, as is the **Stock Exchange Official Year Book** which lists companies quoted on the Stock Exchange. The **Directory of Directors** and **Who's Who** may be useful in finding out more about Company Directors. These and other publications may well be available in your local Reference Library. For local companies, you should use a combination of **A Guide to Company Giving**, the appropriate regional section of **Kompass** and lists of firms from the local Chamber of Commerce. Other sources include the local authority Economic Development department or Rating department, which may have a list of larger local employers or ratepayers. The Business in the Community **Directory of Enterprise Agencies** lists local enterprise agencies together with their sponsors, which is a good list of locally concerned companies. There is your own local knowledge of the area. The **Yellow Pages** is a useful supplement for smaller firms.

If you want gifts in kind, you will want to find likely suppliers of what you need. Where there is a trade association, the association will often provide a list of its member companies. Another idea is trade exhibition catalogues which will give details of all exhibitors.

Directories and lists are often out of date. If you have time and think it is worth expending the effort, telephone the companies and ask if the details you have are correct, for example the Managing Director's name.

One big problem is the ownership of seemingly independent companies. Many companies are in fact a part of a much larger concern, and in recent years there have been very substantial numbers of mergers and take-overs as well as the buying and selling of business between corporations. One source of information is the directory **Who Owns Whom**. You can also use company annual reports, which (for most companies) it is possible to obtain on request from the Company Secretary. These reports provide good background information on the company, and may also provide some information on the company's charitable support programme. Some private companies, and the occasional public company will not be prepared to send out its annual reports except to shareholders. In such cases you can go to Companies House to get hold of a copy (if you really must have one).

Finally, there are national and local newspapers which can provide you with useful information and ideas about who to approach. If a company is about to start up or to close down in an area, this may provide opportunities for giving support locally.

Raising money locally

A local charity will adopt a rather different strategy in its approach to companies than a national charity. Although you can appeal to the larger national companies, generally speaking such an appeal will only have a chance of success if there is some **'product link'** (where what the charity does somehow can be linked to what the company does), or if there is some **'geographical link'** (perhaps the company's Head Office, a large factory or a subsidiary company is in your area). But there are other opportunities:

1. Local branches of national companies

Some very large donors including the high street banks and some multiple stores give through their local branches. The amounts that can be given without having to be submitted to Head Office for approval are usually very much smaller than for national donations. But the money is there. Some companies like to support charities which their staff are involved in. So if you have a volunteer who works for the *National Westminster Bank*, say, then ask him whether you can apply to his Regional Office for a donation. Some of the very large donors which do not have a branch structure, make smallish amounts of money available to local charities in those areas where they have a presence through their local subsidiaries or plants.

2. Large donors who give locally

Some companies have moved to being predominately local givers. For example *Allied Dunbar* gives substantially in the Swindon area where it is based, and *J Rothschild Holdings* gives a part of its budget to local projects in Central London. The independent TV companies tend to give substantially in their franchise area. Some research into the donations policies of large companies in your area will provide a starting point. If you find that none are giving locally at the moment, then perhaps you should think about persuading them to change to doing so.

3. Local companies

There are a myriad of companies that make up the local business community. Although these may be a power in your local community, they may not be quoted on the Stock Exchange or have any national presence. These vary from companies employing a few hundred to those employing just a few. The local business community will have its own networks including the *Chamber of Commerce*, the *Rotary Club* and the *Masonic Lodge*. You will need to think carefully about how to reach these firms, and who you might enlist to help you to do so. You can find out who to approach from some of the sources we have already listed, or from your own local knowledge. You might even consider going door-to-door down the local high street or trading estate, particularly if you are seeking gifts in kind.

4. Companies you have some existing contact with

If you have or can create personal contacts, then those companies will be worth approaching. Other ideas are to appeal to your suppliers: this will include your bank, solicitors, accountants as well as those companies that supply you with goods. Always mention the fact that you are a valued customer. If you are a local charity you would appeal to your bank via its Regional Office. Your accountants or solicitors may also be able to provide useful contacts; some charities even appoint advisers who have good business connections, which they can then bring in when they need to raise money.

Many local firms may find it easier to make you a gift in kind or pay for advertising space in a brochure (indeed a whole industry of telephone selling of advertising space in diaries and brochures on commission now seems to have grown up and is occasionally 'exposed' in the national press). So don't just think in terms of cash donations. Decide what you want and what these companies might be persuaded to give you. Even make a 'shopping list' of your needs, and then think about who to approach for what.

Remember that if you have a strong belief in the importance of what you are doing, then nobody is too small to approach. It is a matter of time, patience and persuasion – and of getting the right person to do the persuading. If you can get some publicity in the local press, then this too can be an incentive in persuading local companies to give.

The approach

Be clear about why you need the money. It is important to be clear about the objectives of the work you are raising money for, about its time scale, and about how it relates to your overall programme of work. You should try to think in project terms or seek support for some specific item of expenditure, rather than asking for a contribution towards your basic administration costs – this can be difficult, because most people spend most of their money on administration in one form or another. You need to try to conjure up projects out of what you are doing to present to potential donors. It is a real skill to come up with ideas and activities which catch the imagination of the donor. Remember that the business sector may find it easier to fund some things than others; for example, support for an addiction treatment centre would be less

less likely than support for a series of leaflets to be used in schools.

It is also very important how you 'sell' yourself. You need very crisp and very clear applications, and you need to read through them carefully to see that they make sense and that they are not cluttered up with jargon. Government bodies, both central and local, and to a certain extent trusts, are bureaucratic machines able to digest reams of descriptive analysis of what you are doing and what you hope to achieve. Industry is much less of a paper machine, so you should confine what you put in your application to the essence of what you are doing. If you are longwinded, hazy or unclear, it will not help you.

Be persistent. Do not underestimate the factor of persistence. If you do not receive a donation in the first year, do not take that as an indication that they will never support you. Go back again a second time and even a third time.

If you are going back again, you can mention the fact that you have applied to them previously, perhaps saying that you are now presenting them with something different which may be (you hope) of more interest to them.

If they give you reasons why they are refusing you, then use these reasons to help you put in more appropriate applications in the future. If they said that they do not give to your particular type of activity, then you know that it is absolutely no use your going back. If they said that their funds were fully committed, you can try to find out when would be a better time to apply (although this might only have been a convenient excuse because they did not want to support you).

Note any response to your appeal on a card index, and use any information you can glean to improve your chances the next time. People respect persistence, so it really is important to go back again and again.

The more direct the approach, the more likely you are to get your case across. Here are a number of different ways of making an appeal, listed in order of persuasiveness:

An individual approach or face-to-face discussion.

A meeting or presentation for a group of potential donors.

A telephone call.

An individual letter.

A circular letter.

Other techniques such as a telex or fax appeal or sending a pre-recorded tape of the appeal are not yet widely acceptable, and the recipient may feel you are wasting your money or being tricksy.

Where you have the opportunity to make your case face-to-face, then do so. Few companies have the time or inclination to visit projects or see applicant charities, but it may be possible to secure a meeting, if your organisation is seen as being important or if there is a good reason.

Equally it may be possible to ring up 'out of the blue' if there is some urgency or a specific request you are making (such as for a gift in kind). For example, Help the Aged asked its regional organisers to raise money in the freezing winter of 1986/87 by asking people to look out of the window and telling them about the problems of old people and hypothermia, and the local needs.

Normally for a smaller or unknown organisation, it is better to put your case in writing first, and then, if you feel it is worthwhile, seek a meeting or follow up the letter with a phone call.

Another possibility is to arrange a meeting, open day or site visit. If the event is sponsored, or someone prominent is hosting the occasion, then this can work well. Such events do need to be followed up subsequently if they are to produce results.

Some key factors

Lastly some points which are important for you to consider when you are constructing your appeal letter:

● Try to think up a project or aspect of your work that the business sector might like to support. Generally do not appeal for administration costs or a contribution to an endowment fund (although there will be cases where this approach will succeed). Recognise that companies are likely to be interested in some things and not others. An appreciation of the kind of things that companies will like to support will be very helpful to you.

● Your letter should be as short as possible. Try to get it all on one side of a piece of paper if you can. You can always supply further information as attachments to the appeal letter. Company people are busy. They already receive too many appeals. You can help them by making your appeal short and to the point. It should be written clearly and concisely and be free from jargon. A person not acquainted with what you are doing should be able to read it and understand it and be persuaded to act on it. So perhaps give your letter in draft to someone else to read and to comment on before finalising it and sending it out.

● You should state why you need the money and how exactly it will be spent. The letter itself should be straightforward. It should include the following information (not necessarily in this order): what the organisation does, and some background on how it was set up; why its work is important; why the organisation needs funds; how the donation would be spent if it were to be forthcoming; and why you think the company might be interested in supporting you.

● You should attempt to communicate a sense of urgency in your appeal. Fund-raising is an intensely competitive business – there is a limited amount of money to give away, and you have to ensure that some of it comes your way. So if it appears that, although you would like the money now, it would not matter terribly much if you got it next year, this would tend to put people off. You should also try to show that your charity is well-run, efficient and cost-effective in how it operates.

● You should mention *why* you think the company should support your cause. This could range from rather generalised notions of corporate responsibility and the creation of goodwill in the local community, to much more specific advantages, for example, preventing children painting graffiti on their factory walls or the good publicity they will get from helping you. If there is likely to be any publicity arising from the gift, then emphasise the goodwill which will accrue to the company. Most companies would say publicly that you do not require any public acknowledgement for the charitable contributions they make, but most will in fact appreciate and welcome this.

● Ask for something specific. It is all too easy to make a good case and then to mumble something about needing money and being grateful for any support they might care to give. Many companies, having been persuaded to give, are not sure how much to give. You can ask them to give a donation of a specific amount (matched to what you believe their ability to contribute to be), or to contribute the cost of a particular item. You can suggest a figure by mentioning what other companies are giving. You can mention a total and say how many donations you will need to achieve this. Don't be unreasonable in your expectations. Just because a company is large and rich, that doesn't mean that it makes big grants. If you have information on the company's grant range that will be helpful. If not, then look at the companies annual total donations figure, and make a reasonable inference.

● If you can demonstrate some form of 'leverage' this will be an added attraction. Company donations, on the whole are quite modest, and companies like to feel they are having a substantial impact with the money they spend. This is one reason why some are reluctant to support large national appeals. If you can show that a small amount of money will enable a much larger project to go ahead, or will release further funds say on a matching basis from another source, this will definitely be an advantage.

● Stress your success. If you have been successful in running projects, getting grants, getting support from other companies, getting media coverage, then mention this. Everyone prefers to back a winner rather than a loser.

● Having written a very short appeal letter, you can append some background support literature. This should not be a fifty-page treatise outlining your latest policies, but like your letter it should be crisp and to the point, a record of your achievements, your latest annual report, or even a specially produced brochure to accompany your appeal.

● Make sure that the letter is addressed to the correct person at the correct address. This is the background research work you will need to do. If you are appealing to industry in any serious way, it is always worth doing this work. Use the various trade directories, business information services or Yellow Pages as appropriate, and use the telephone to find out or confirm who to send your letter to. Keep all the information on file, as this will make your job much easier next time around.

How to write a good application

The function of the application is to get the support you are looking for. There is no one best way of making an appeal. What works for you is what you should be doing. As you get more experienced, you should be able to improve your performance. Here are some points to bear in mind:

In your application, you must make a good case for support. That goes without saying. But. . . .

You must also try to answer all the reasons they may conjure up for rejecting your application. 'We've never heard of them.' 'There are too many charities all doing the same thing.' 'What they are doing is not really important.' 'Someone else should be paying the cost.' 'They are inefficient.' 'Our donation would be insignificant.' 'Why us?' and so on.

Before making the approach, you should feel that there is at least some chance that they will help you target your appeal on likely supporters. You will also highlight any special reasons why they might be interested in your appeal. They may not realise why, so telling them helps. This approach will work far better than sending a circular appeal to the top 500 or 1,000 companies.

Style and content

Applications to companies should be:

● **Short**. Try to put everything on one side of an A4 sheet of paper. They are busy people and they only need sufficient information to make a decision. If they want more details, they will get in touch with you.

● **Concise** and **clear.** Within the limited space available, you need to state your case for support, not pad out your letter with waffle, jargon, long sentences or long words.

● **Positive** and **upbeat.** People like to support success not failure.

● **Professionally competent.** Nicely typed on not-too-scruffy writing paper, wherever possible.

● **Not too lavish.** Glossy brochures are only appropriate for large prestigious national and local appeals. In all other circumstances, glossiness can work against you, as it gives the hidden message that you are wasting money. If you do have to have an expensive brochure, get it sponsored and show this prominently. This shows good housekeeping and that you have already been successful.

● **Individually addressed** to the company. Most circular appeals are thrown in the bin. Try to write an individual letter to each company, addressed to a named person in the company. Word processors can help, but it helps if the letter does not look word processed. Topping and tailing a prepared letter is an alternative, matching in the addressee's name and address and the 'Dear . . .' salutation using the same typeface as for the body text of the letter.

The application should state:

● **Who** you are and **what** you do.

● **What** the problem is and **why** it is important.

● **What** your organisation is proposing to do about the problem, and **why** it is significant.

● **What** you need the money for, and **how much** you need.

● **What** you are asking the company to give. Also state any leverage effect – how their (small) contribution will achieve a large amount of action or impact, or how it will help you.

● **Why** the company might be interested in giving its support. Tell them the reasons why. Don't assume that they will realise it for themselves.

● **Enclosures:** Attach to your letter anything which you feel will enhance your appeal. Last annual accounts, a brochure, a letter of commendation, etc.

The addressee and signatory are also important:

The letter should be addressed to **a named individual** in the company, with the correct job title. Letters that start 'Dear Sir' or 'Dear Sir or Madam' or ones which are sent to someone who left the company many years ago will all get your appeal off on the wrong foot. The *Guide to Company Giving* lists the appropriate contacts for large companies. If you feel that your appeal stands a good chance, then it may be worth checking, where the information is not fully up-to-date.

The individual should be the person who deals with the company's appeal mail or who is responsible for making the decision. Remember that different people may have different responsibilities within the same large company. There may be someone who deals with donations, someone else who deals with corporate sponsorship, and yet others who deal with sponsorship which promotes sales of company products. A branch manager may be able to make small donations to local charities, a regional manager or director of a subsidiary may be able to make grants within certain guidelines. At head office, sponsorship may be decided completely separately from donations, or there may be one department dealing with everything. If you know the Chairman or Managing Director personally, than you can always address your appeal personally to them.

The signatory can also be important. A prominent local or national businessman who chairs your Appeal Committee or who is writing on your behalf will carry great clout, and is harder to refuse (especially if the asking is done in person). An Administrative Assistant or Appeals Officer signing the letter will appear to give the appeal less importance than the Chairman or Director of the charity.

Some donors examine your letterhead to see who they know amongst your patrons and trustees, and this can be a plus factor in deciding a grant. If you need to raise money from business, this is one way of improving your chances.

Making a Good Case

● **Ask for something specific.** The whole point of your appeal is to ask for something. It is far better to be specific in your request, than simply to ask for a 'generous contribution.' If you are not specific, they will have to make two decisions: firstly to support you, and then to decide the size of their contribution. It is far easier if you give some guidance on how much they are expected to give you or how much other similar companies will be giving. You can mention a specific figure. If possible match this amount to some specific achievement or outcome or to the cost of a particular item of expenditure (something that will appear attractive to the donor). You could provide a 'shopping list' of different-sized expenditures for them to choose from. It is up to you to work out the best way of framing your request, and the size of the donation you might expect. This will depend partly on what you need the money for, partly on the sort of charity you are, and partly on the size of the company and your donations budget. If a company gives a total of only £2,000 annually, it is unlikely to contribute a four figure sum, except in the most exceptional circumstances. For larger companies, £10,000 is an exceptional donation, £2,500 would be considered a very gener-ous donation, £1,000–£500 would be what a reputable national organisation might expect to be given, £500–£100 would be a possible range for local appeals.

● **Give reasons for asking.** When applying to a company (but not when applying to a grant-making trust), it will usually be helpful to give a reason or reasons for why you have decided to approach them and why they might want to support your appeal. This will highlight the factors which might help them make up their mind. The reasons why companies give have been discussed in another section. But here are some of the points you might bear in mind.

(a) **Local factors:** The company is based as a large employer in your area.

(b) **Product link:** Your work is somehow connected with the company's business, or deals with problems that particularly concern the company.

(c) **Return for the company:** The company will gain somehow from being associated with your project. This will obviously be critical for a sponsorship proposal, when you will list all the benefits that the company might expect, but even when you are asking for a donation the company may be interested in any local or national publicity that might accrue.

(d) **Employee link:** If a member of the company's staff is involved in your work in some way (for example, on the Committee, as a volunteer, or in raising money), this should be mentioned. Most companies give some preference to appeals in which a member of staff is involved, and this could be the deciding factor.

(e) **Previous Contact:** If you have received support before, mention it. They might like to support you again.

(f) **Personal contact:** Many donations are still made through personal contact, and this will be particularly the case for smaller companies. If you have a genuine personal contact with the company right at the top, then this may be the key factor in getting support. But sending a letter might not be the best way of going about it.

(g) **Other support:** Companies like to know which other companies are supporting you. This can provide reassurance, and some companies like to match the donations their colleagues or competitors are making.

These are some of the main points to bear in mind when writing an appeal letter to companies. We will illustrate these points further with actual examples. On the following pages we are reproducing some letters sent by various charities with our comments on how they might be 'improved'.

Remember, though, that a good appeal letter is not everything. You need to be running a good project meeting an evident need; the cause or issue needs to be something that is likely to attract company support; it helps if your organisation is well-known or has prominent trustees, and your accounts should demonstrate a competence in handling money.

EXAMPLE 1

An appeal letter from a local arts project in East London.

Ansett Airlines

Heathcoat Ho

Saville Row

W1

16th September

Dears Sirs

This request comes to ask for your help in any way possible.

_____ Arts Development Company is a charitable educational/cultural arts organisation, formed in November, 1982; to act as a resource and outlet for the community.

Our present centre is an eight track recording studio cum rehearsal room, which gives access to numerous groups and organisations. Our range of music extends from running I.T. Courses for young offenders, to organising festivals, teaching recording engineering and recording young artists.

_____ also runs several educational workshops (viz: jazz, dance, drumming, conga/percussion, beginner's music, drama etc.); which currently takes place in other clubs and centres, as there is insufficient room at the studio for any other activity to function. For this reason, we have been awarded a spacious building in London E8, which we are currently making plans to move into. Hence our appeal to your company.

We are desperately in need of funds to renovate our new building, thus bringing it to a state consistent with its intended use as an arts/cultural centre for the community.

Funds would go towards a feasability study, building/renovation costs, professional fees and administrative costs etc.

Our architects have estimated a total sum of £400,000 for this project. To date, we have been allocated £8,300 from the _____ Trust, to help towards the first phase of the building works.

We ask that you consider our appeal and help us in any way possible.

We would be pleased to send you further information, if required.

Thanking you for your kind consideration.

Yours faithfully,

M J _____

ADMINISTRATOR

This letter contains a number of basic mistakes.

1. There is no apparent connection between the project and the company. Why should an Australian-owned airline want to make a cash donation to a Hackney arts project? The only reason given is that 'we are desperately in need of funds.'

2. There is a mismatch between scale of the need as related to the ability of the company to contribute. A total of £400,000 is required, out of which only £8,300 has been promised so far. In order for such an appeal to be successful, the applicant would need to indicate where the bulk of the money is likely to come from and to suggest a target for company support within the overall appeal budget. The main part of the support should be secured before approaching smaller donors.

3. Try to ask for something specific or a specific amount. It is easier to have only one decision to make, yes or no. So if you suggest that you are seeking 25 contributions of £1,000 from companies or state that _____ company has agreed to contribute £2,500 which suggests a level for the company to pitch its giving at, or to provide a shopping list of items of a range of values. Alternatively a 'shopping list' of specific items for which support is being sought, for example, the cost of buying furniture or renovating a room gives an indication that the appeal has been closely thought out. If you do provide a shopping list, make the items sound relevant, attractive and good value.

4. Always send a letter to a named individual. 'Dear Sir' suggests that you have not taken sufficient trouble to find out who to write to. If it is worth making an approach, it is almost certainly worth telephoning first to find out who deals with appeals in the name of the chairman.

The fate of this letter is almost certainly to be consigned to the wastepaper basket. Any applicant should aim to do better than that.

EXAMPLE 2

An appeal letter from a university library appeal,

which would be personalised with the recipient's name/address and
sent with an accompanying brochure.

Dear (*name of donor*)

I am writing to ask if you could help the _____
College Library Appeal Fund.

_____ College is a unique institution in British
higher education. Its 3,000 or so full-time and about 5,000 part-time
students do a variety of degree and postgraduate courses. The College
is especially renowned for its work in adult education, teacher training
and the visual and performing arts.

The Department of Education and science has decided that the present
College Library is woefully inadequate, both in terms of book space and
working space, and is substantially funding the cost of a new library.
However, the College itself has to find £1,000,000. This we are doing by
the sale of certain properties and by appeals to charitable trusts,
businesses and private individuals. The College itself has almost no
private resources. It is the only university institution south of
_____ and is the largest employer in the region.

We are making this appeal on environmental, as much as an academic
grounds, and it is for this reason that I am writing to ask for your help.
_____ is a very desolate area and we feel that the
College, with its close local ties (we offer Adult Literacy and Open
Access courses) and its work in the field of Visual and Performing Arts
acts as a civilising influence. Certainly our part-time adult evening
students bring life and spending power to a most deprived area.

As we are not in a social funding area, we do not qualify for European
help and we are just too far removed to get money from the
Development Corporation.

So far, donations have ranged from £100,000 to £5 and the college really
would be most grateful if you could see your way to helping by making
a donation or a covenant.

If you would like to visit the College we would be delighted to show
you something of our work. I do hope you can help.

Yours sincerely,

D_____ R_____.
Secretary to the Library Appeal.

This is a much better letter. A good, clear and concise case has been made. It differs from the previous example, in that, as a prestigious institution the applicant needs to spend less time explaining itself and its work, which leaves more space to make a good case. But even a good letter can be improved. The main points here are:

1. Give a clear financial picture. How much of the total appeal target will be raised by the sale of properties which should provide a substantial chunk. A paragraph such as the following could be included:

> The present College Library is woefully inadequate both in terms of book space and working space. The College has decided that it has to build a new library. This will cost a total of £____ million. The Department of Education and Science is putting up £____ million of the funds, but the College itself must raise the balance of £1 million. Of this, £____ will be raised through the sale of certain properties, and we also plan to raise £____ from private individuals and £____ from an appeal to trusts and companies.

This also suggests that the decision is the College's, and not the DES, which is better because it shows the College taking the initiative rather than responding to outside pressures.

2. Build on the particular concerns and interests of business. This letter has a relevance to very local companies who all share in the economic success of the neighbourhood. Other companies may be interested in the skills shortage, school-industry links, technical education, training schemes run in conjunction with companies, etc. One letter will not do for all donors.

3. The European Social Fund does not support library appeals; it is a programme to give support to projects providing training and retraining for work. It is a red herring to mention this.

4. A more specific amount could be asked for (as in example 1).

5. The appeal had an extemely prestigious Appeal Committee. What were they doing and why was the appeal signed by the Appeal Secretary? At least, the appeal could have been signed by a Committee member. But more than this, a written appeal letter requesting a donation may not be the best approach. Personal contact with likely companies, a reception to launch the business appeal, certainly an attempt at telephone contact to build on the written communication are all worth considering. The answer to a financial need may not simply be to fire off correctly addressed, well-written appeal letters.

EXAMPLE 3

An appeal letter from a London-based Marriage Guidance Council.

Mr R W Jenkins
25 Milk Street
London EC2V 8LU

14th August

Dear Mr Jenkins

re: T S B Social & Community Welfare Foundation.

I would be most grateful if you would consider the details below as worthy of a grant.

_____ Marriage Guidance Council covers the four London boroughs of _____.
Just over 40% of our day to day running costs are provided by grants from these four boroughs with the rest coming from client contributions and local fund-raising efforts. Our administrative and professional costs are kept very low due to a large voluntary workforce who give a dedicated service. A simple division of our total expenditure last year by the total number of hours output by our counsellors gives a unit cost of under £4.50 per hour. We are however facing an increasing crisis threatening the validity of our work and our financial viability.

Over the past four years our counselling workforce has been reduced from 50 to 40, a reduction of 20%. This has been due to retirement or to moving. This is despite a growing demand for all four branches of our service: remedial counselling, sexual therapy, education and training and family mediation. Our waiting list currently stands at 380, comprised of single people, couples and families, which means a wait of between 2 to 6 months depending on when they are available to be seen. For many this is proving too long with disastrous consequences. The waiting list is growing at an alarming rate. The hub of our problem is this. A fully trained counsellor currently costs us £2,000 to train over a two year period. All our statutory grants and donations only provide for the maintenance of our existing service, they do not provide for a turnover of counsellors or for growth. To get back to our counselling output of four years ago we require another ten new counsellors costing us £20,000 in training costs. To reach the nationally researched target of 10 counsellors per 10,000 population, thus giving a zero waiting list, we require an extra 60 counsellors costing £120,000. We have approached our local authorities concerning this but have been unsuccessful. Indeed as two of our local authorities are to be rate-capped next year, we face the prospect of a reduced grant income rather than any increases.

Marriage Guidance Councils have an unfashionable profile for fund-raising. We don't specifically combat unemployment, homelessness, inner city blight, abused children or any of the popular causes. That view is however very shallow. Our contribution to society's hardship that we help alleviate is immeasurable and vitally important. Our work is increasingly involving children especially in our Family Mediation Work. Before dismissing this appeal out of hand or deciding it doesn't fit any priority category, please do take time to consider the plight of the many thousands of families who would literally have no one to turn to if we were not here.

Thank you for your time in considering this appeal. If you require further information, I would be happy to provide it.

Yours sincerely,

S C
DIRECTOR

The following improvements are suggested:

1. The first lines of the appeal can be discarded. Re: T S B Social and Community Welfare Foundation can be incorporated into the address; in any case the letter is re: a marriage guidance appeal. The first sentence is pompous in an old-fashioned way, and does not add anything to the appeal.

2. The appeal should highlight success rather than dwell on failure. The fact that there has been a 20% reduction in service despite a growth in need, need not be mentioned. Nor need next year's rate capping. What is required are trained counsellors at a specific cost to help more families, the donor will not want to be involved in all your problems, only in those which he can help you solve.

3. Pitch the aspiration at what is immediately achievable. The suggestion that 60 new counsellors are needed at a cost of

£120,000 really only highlights a failure of the Council to meet demands for its service. Why not keep the initial objective to training 10 new counsellors at a cost of £20,000. This would make a much more donor-friendly target, and the TSB could decide to give one or more units of £2,000.

4. 'The distress and hardship that we help alleviate is immeasurable . . .'. No, it is not. It can be measured. Every cause will be able to draw on simple facts and figures to illustrate and strengthen its case. The consequences of family disruption particularly on family incomes and the effect on children are now well documented, and it could be argued with confidence that Marriage Guidance Councils are dealing with one of the serious social problems of our age. The aim is to produce a well-argued case backed up with factual information and statistics, and try to avoid loose phrases such as 'vast contribution', 'immeasurable' or overused words such as 'unique', 'desperate', 'urgent', which are emotive but unspecific.

5. A division of expenditure by counsellor output gives a unit cost of £4.50 per hour. The figure is not particularly meaningful to the reader. Two pieces of information might be more interesting. Firstly, the number of volunteer hours contributed by an average counsellor each year, and the total volunteer input for the Council as a whole. This gives an indication of 'leverage', how a small amount of money put into training or administration will liberate a much larger amount of professional resources to be applied to the problem. And secondly, the cost per family counselled, which could be compared to the social and other costs of not providing help at a crucial stage of family breakdown.

6. Remember there are Marriage Guidance Councils all over Britain. Any special factors affecting the particular Council or the area it is operating in, or any pioneering approaches to its work could be highlighted to show a specially deserving case or important cause.

Which companies to approach

There are over one million companies on the Companies Register, and although many are shell companies, others have ceased or not yet started trading, and others very small, it does leave a lot of companies as a potential target for your fund-raising. The art of the successful fund-raiser is to approach those companies that are going to say yes and not to waste time on those that will say no. This means that you will have to try to identify those companies which are likely to be interested in your appeal.

The procedure for doing this is *research* leading to the compilation of a *list* of likely prospects. There are two factors to take into account: the size of the company and how this matches the nature of your own activities, and what you are seeking the money for (which affects the sorts of company that will be interested in supporting you).

1. Size

British business is very highly centralised. The top companies are major business combines owning and operating subsidiaries in a variety of businesses. What may appear a small independent company may well turn out to be part of a multinational combine.

The top 200 companies give £63.3 million to charity and this probably represents about 50% of all cash donations to charity made by businesses. So one method of beginning your research is to consult the list of top companies. *The Times 1000* and *Business Magazine 500* (both published annually) give details of leading companies. *Charity Trends* (published annually by the Charities Aid Foundation) lists the top 400 corporate donors. *A Guide to Company Giving* (published by the Directory of Social Change) gives information and statistics on the giving of the top 1,300 corporate donors; this information is supplemented by the companion book *Major Companies and their Charitable Giving*, which gives more detail on the top 350 companies. These lists provide a good starting point and much additional information for approaching the larger companies. There are, of course, many other companies which give or could give generously. Indeed, those companies which do not appear on any of these various lists but which you can research and identify for yourself are less likely to be known to others, and being less known, will be less approached – and being less approached may be more likely to say yes.

2. Nature of the company

The second stage is to determine whether the company is likely to be interested in your appeal.

In the sections that follow, we discuss three factors which might lead you to believe that the company might be interested, and using these you can decide whether to make an approach and how to frame your appeal.

A *business link*, where the nature of the company's business activity might create an interest in supporting the sort of work you are doing.

A *geographical link*, where the location of the company, its head office, its main plant locations and its local branches provides a match between your local activity and a local presence of the company.

A *personal link*, where you know or are known to the company. There may be other links. For example, the chairman may have attended the school or university or his niece may be suffering from the condition you are combating or his son may be helping a local project as a volunteer. The point is, if you can build some link between you (the charity) and the company, some rationale as to why they should support you, then you will be more likely to be successful.

The better the links, the more interested the company is likely to be, and the larger the grant you can expect. A good example is the *Dundee Heritage Trust* which has been running an appeal to create a textile industry museum. The *Sidlaw Group* made a contribution of £40,000 towards this appeal via a deed of covenant. Sidlaw Group is an industrial company involved in oil services and textiles. It is one of the few large companies based in Dundee. And almost certainly there will be some personal involvement with the museum project. Sidlaw would obviously be one of the major 'targets' for this appeal, and one that should be approached first, as a lead donor.

An example showing who has given

The following is a list of business donors to a Northern university appeal. A great deal of effort went into securing these 28 donations totalling £57,830. If the applicant had been able to know in advance which companies were going to give or could be persuaded to give, and which companies were not interested, it would make the fund-raising that much easier. The art is to determine for yourself which are the most likely companies to want to give to your organisation, and to concentrate your efforts on those, whilst not necessarily ignoring other companies.

Artix Ltd	4,830
Barclays Bank plc	5,000
Bellway plc	600
British Telecommunications	500
Charterhouse Bank Ltd	250
Compass Services	500
J Dinesley & Son	200
Ecclesiastical Insurance Office	1,750
Gerrard & National plc	250
Imperial Chemical Industries plc	5,000
Lloyds Bank plc	1,000
London & Northern Group plc	250
Manufacturers Hanover Trust	1,000
National Westminster Bank plc	1,000
Northern Clubs Federation Brewery	685
Northern Engineering Industries plc	1,000
Pattison & Co	660
Peninsular & Orient Steam Navigation Co plc	500
Republic National Bank of New York	27,400

N M Rothschild and Sons	400
Scottish and Newcastle Brewery	1,500
Seagram UK Ltd	1,000
Security Pacific Holdings Ltd	1,380
TSB	1,000
Edwin Turner Ltd	25
Tyne Tees Television Holding plc	500
Union Discount Co of London	400
Wise Speke Ltd	250

Business links

The nature of the company's business can have a significant impact on the charitable concerns and involvement of the company. The creative grant-seeker will try to build these into the approach, thereby giving more persuasive reasons why the appeal should be supported.

Sometimes these links are little more than a device in the game of grant-seeking. For example, there is no really good reason why a building products supplier or a housebuilder or a property developer might want to support a hostel project for the homeless, but a link can be made which makes supporting this kind of appeal appear logical.

Occasionally there are very real concerns of business which match the concerns of charities. Here a natural partnership can be forged to solve or deal with a common problem. A good example of this is the large grant made by *Citicorp* (the New York based bank with a large UK financial services operation) to the Greater London Citizens Advice Bureaux for debt counselling/money advice work. Another is the partnership of *Shell UK* with the British Trust for Conservation Volunteers, the Nature Conservancy Council and other conservation bodies in the Shell Better Britain Campaign promoting a better environment through information, advice, awards and grants for local action. A third is the support given by *ARC* (a subsidiary of Consolidated Goldfields) through the Gold Fields Trust to the environmental improvement of its worked out gravel pits (this policy has now changed emphasis to stimulate rural enterprise in areas of ARC operations). There will inevitably be cases where the company is seen as the problem creator, and it would be inappropriate for the charity to receive a grant or develop a close working partnership with the company. Alcohol advice projects might be reluctant to accept support from a brewer, a heart or health charity from a tobacco company, or a Third World charity from an international arms supplier. It is up to each and every charity to think about and decide the categories of company it does not wish to receive support from, bearing in mind its own outlook, the range of its activities, and the attitudes of its members and other supporters. It is important to get this ethical dimension of company giving straightened out *before* making an approach.

At the end of this section we list the major donors (the top 165 companies all of which give £100,000 or more to charity) categorised by nature of their business activity.

There are three further aspects of business links which are worth considering:

● **Name Identity:** If there is a link between the name of your project or event and the company, then this can provide a good basis for support. In Seattle, USA, the opera company mounted a season under the banner *'Opera's a Gas!'* and had the season sponsored by an oil major (gas in US parlance). In a similar vein, the Theatre Royal Stratford was working for sponsorship for a play called 'Pork Pies', and approached *Walls Mattesons*. However, pork pies is cockney rhyming slang for lies, and the play was a political play about the Nineteen Eighties. There was no likelihood of a successful sponsorship, and the object of the approach was probably to show the Arts Council that sponsorship could interfere with artistic or editorial integrity. An example that worked was the Portsmouth City Art Gallery show called 'Stop the Rot' which was given £3,000 by *Rentokil* and even won an award for first time sponsorship under the government's Business Sponsorship Incentive Scheme.

● **Sponsorship:** Unlike a donation which does not seek a business return, the whole purpose of sponsorship is the return that the company can obtain as a result of its financial support. Here the key to getting support is to list the returns available and to ensure that they make an attractive proposition for the company. Sponsorship has been described and discussed in *Part 1* of this book.

● **A business service:** Many charities, because of their particular cause or expertise, may be in a good position to provide some form of professional service to a company on a business basis for a fee. Such money would come out of the appropriate budget and what might be quite substantial support for the charity could be a relatively trivial expenditure for the company.

Ideas and examples could include: the provision of day care or creche facilities for staff and customers (workforce daycare is big in the USA, and could become more important here as companies compete for a declining labour force); counselling for pre-retirement or employment-linked problems such as stress or alcoholism; opportunities for keep fit or outdoor venture experiences; education and training modules for Employment Training and Youth Training programmes; advice on equal opportunity hiring, or an AIDS policy; relocation advice and welcome manuals for companies moving head office; and so on.

As we move into the 1990's, the 1970's approach to funding, by seeking grant-aided support and subsidy, which persisted throughout the 1980's despite social changes and the increasingly fierce competition for available funds, is likely to be supplanted by a more survivalist approach, with more emphasis on creative approaches to balancing the charity budget. Employers and the employed offer a vast market for charities to sell their services enabling them at the same time to fight the causes or meet the real social needs for which they were established.

Where to get information

Suppose you are a children's charity and wish to approach companies involved in making or selling children's clothes, foods, toys, books, educational materials, where do you find out the names and addresses of leading companies in these categories. There are a number of possibilities:

● **Trade associations/professional bodies:** in most trades there are business associations established to promote the interests of members. These often publish trade directories or yearbooks which give details of member's companies.

● **Trade fairs:** Where there is a trade fair, there is likely to be a catalogue of exhibitors, with details of who and how to contact.

● **Specialist magazines:** There include consumer magazines covering every interest from angling to zoology, all of which will contain some advertising by suppliers, as well as trade magazines and journals.

There are also a number of agencies promoting company community involvement which might also be able to suggest likely companies, particularly **Business in the Community** which promotes company community involvement generally and the **Association for Business Sponsorship of the Arts** which keeps a register of sponsorship opportunities for its member companies and others seeking its advice.

Companies which give more than £100,000 per annum to charity classified by nature of company business and in order of donations total within each category

Banking/Finance

TSB Group
Barclays
National Westminster
Midland
Lloyds
S G Warburg
Royal Bank of Scotland
British and Commonwealth
Standard Chartered
J Rothschild Holdings
3i Group

Bank of Scotland
N M Rothschild & Sons
Nationwide Anglia
Abbey National
Kleinwort Benson Lonsdale
Bank of England
Schroders
Phibro-Saloman
Hill Samuel
Morgan Grenfell Group
Hambros

(*Note:* Barings Bank is wholly owned by the Baring Foundation, the M & G unit trust group is substantially owned by the Esmée Fairbairn Charitable Trust, both of which are big donors).

Brewing

Bass
Whitbread
Vaux

Guinness
Scottish & Newcastle Breweries
Seagram Holdings

Chemicals/Drugs

Imperial Chemical Industries
BOC Group
Glaxo Holdings
Beecham Group

Smith & Nephew Associated Co
Wellcome
Merck Sharpe & Dohme
Courtaulds

(*Note:* The Wellcome Foundation is 75% owned by the Wellcome Trust, which is the UK's single largest grant-making foundation, and whose donations programme is operated separately from the Company's.)

Construction/Building Products

Consolidated Gold Fields (ARC)
BPB Industries

Blue Circle Industries

(*Note:* the Wimpey building company is substantially owned by the Tudor Trust, and the John Laing building company is substantially owned by four Laing charitable foundations.)

Electronics/Electrical

IBM United Kingdom Holdings
STC
General Electric Company
Lucas Industries
Plessey Company

Hewlett Packard
Rank Xerox
Racal Electronics
Thorn EMI

Food and Consumer Goods

Unilever
Grand Metropolitan
United Biscuits (Holdings)
S & W Beresford
Allied Lyons
Dalgety
Rowntree
Kellogg Company
Northern Foods

Tate & Lyle
Food Manufacturers (GB Co)
Ranks Hovis McDougall
Cadbury Schweppes
Reckitt & Colman
Johnson Wax
H J Heinz Co
Associated British Foods

(*Note:* Rowntree was taken over by Nestles in 1988, but retains its own separate donations programme. Associated British Foods operates from the same address in the Garfield Weston Foundation, which is independent of the company. Food Manufacturers is the Mars confectionery and petfoods group.)

Industrial

BICC
Rover Group
Pilkington
Ford Motor Co
Vickers
GKN
TI Group
Jaguar

Metal Box
Siebe
Northern Engineering Industries
British Steel Corporation
Kaye Organisation
Hawker Siddely Group
British Alcan Aluminium

(*Note:* The Kaye Organisation, a privately owned company, has now sold its Lansing-Bagenall fork lift truck business.)

Insurance

Prudential Corporation
C T Bowring
Norwich Union
Willis Faber
Guardian Royal Exchange

Legal and General
Commercial Union
Pearl Group
General Accident
Sedgwick Group

(*Note:* Allied Dunbar, which is a subsidiary of BAT Industries, gave £925,000 in 1987.)

Oil
British Petroleum Co
Shell UK Ltd
Esso UK

Conoco UK
Burmah Oil

Publishing
Reed International
News International
International Thomson

Pearson
Reuters Holdings
Associated Newspapers

Retail
Marks & Spencer
J Sainsbury
John Lewis Partnership
The Boots Company
Burton Group
Tesco
Sears
W H Smith
Dee Corporation

ASDA Group
Storehouse
Woolworth Holdings
Next
Dixons Group
House of Fraser
Laura Ashley Holdings
C & A Stores

(*Note:* the Sainsbury charitable budget operates in close contact with a number of Sainsbury family trusts, and likewise the C & A stores charitable budget is linked with but independent of the Marble Arch group of charitable trusts.)

Television/radio
Television South
Central Independent Television
Yorkshire Television Holdings
Capital Radio
Anglia Television

Scottish Television
Tyne Tees Television
HTV Group
Thames Television

(*Note:* these and other media companies do raise substantial sums for charity – see *Charities and Broadcasting* published by the Directory of Social Change.)

Tobacco
Hanson Trust
BAT Industries

Rothmans International
Gallaher

(*Note:* these companies include substantial non-tobacco interests. All make large donations to the Health Promotion Research Trust.)

Utilities and transport

British Telecommunications
Cable and Wireless
National Freight Consortium
British Gas

Post Office Group
Peninsular and Orient
British Nuclear Fuels

Sundry

Van Leer (*packaging*)
RTZ (*mining*)
Nissan UK (*motor car distribution*)
Trusthouse Forte (*hotels*)
Heron International (*property, motors, etc*)
Lex Service (*motors etc*)
English China Clays (*extraction*)
PMG Investments (*private company*)
John Swire (*international trading, airlines*)
Coats Viyella (*textiles*)
Sun Hotels (*international hotels*)

Inchcape (*international trading*)
Kodak (*photographic products*)
Christies International (*fine art auctioneers*)
Ladbroke Group (*gaming, hotels, leisure*)
Bunzl (*paper*)
BET (*office services, etc*)
Pirelli (*rubber products*)
Saatchi & Saatchi (*advertising*)
MEPC (*property*)
BTR (*holding company*)
Rank Organisation (*leisure*)

(*Note:* Heron International gives via the Ronson Foundation which owns a very substantial share in the company.)

Geographical links

Where the company and its operations are based can be extremely important in deciding how its charitable budget is spent. In this section, we examine this geographical dimension.

1. National appeals

Most large companies will be prepared to support appeals from national charities out of their head office charitable budgets. The relevance of the appeal, whether there is any personal or employee contact, and how it is presented will all play a part in determining the appeal's success.

However, some companies now prefer not to support large national appeals from 'brand name' charities. They feel that the contribution they can make is so limited that they prefer to give their money where it will have a real impact. A large national charity could seek support for a local project or a specific aspect of their work which might persuade the company to give. There will always be certain appeals which most companies will find it difficult to refuse (such as the Wishing Well Appeal in 1988 for the Great Ormond Street Children's Hospital). A few companies may decide to use their charitable budget only to support local or regional appeals in their main area of operation, and will not want to support general appeals.

2. Local appeals

Most companies will give some preference to local appeals from those areas in which the company has a presence. These are the areas from which they draw their workforce, in which their employees and their families live and in which they will want to build good relationships with the local authority. Being seen as a good corporate citizen in the local community can be important. Equally a company is highly unlikely to want to support local appeals in those areas where it has no business interest or presence.

Local appeals can be made to:

● Large companies with a **head office** based in the area.

● Large companies with a **major plant or subsidiary** in the area.

● Regional companies, that is companies with a **geographically restricted remit** to their operations

● Large companies giving through **local branches**

● Smaller **local companies**

We will examine each of these in turn.

1. Head Office companies

About 50% of all major UK companies have their head office based in the London postal area. Many of these are in the main business districts of the City and the West End. A few of these will have a particular policy of supporting local charities (for example, *Wellcome Foundation* gives some support to the charities in the Euston area).

At the end of this section we list the head office areas for all the top 350 corporate donors which are based outside the London postal area. Not all of these companies will have a policy of supporting local charities, but many will.

A further point to note is the drift of companies to the South East. Many companies once regionally based have moved head office to be nearer the centres of political and financial power. Some companies which once played an important local role have now migrated. Others may have been taken over, often these historical links are recognised through continuing their local support. *Ocean Transport & Trading* (through the P H Holt Charitable Trust) continues to give support in Liverpool although it is now based in London, as does the *Royal Insurance Company* which maintains two important administrative centres in Liverpool. *BP* which took over *Britoil*, made assurances at the time of the takeover that it would highlight the Scottish dimension of its activities, and it has restructured its Scottish grant-making which continues to be substantial. *Guinness*, which took over the Scottish-based *Distillers Company Limited*, has now moved its grant-making administration to Edinburgh. *Rowntree*, which was taken over by *Nestles*, and *Allied Dunbar*, which was taken over by *BAT Industries*, remain substantial givers in York and Swindon respectively.

2. Companies with a major plant presence

Most large companies will allocate a part of their charitable budgets to spend on projects in areas where they have a major presence. Sometimes these budgets are devolved to local management (as with *ICI*). In some cases the decisions are made centrally (as with *Grand Metropolitan*). Either way, if your appeal is sent to the wrong place, it is likely to be forwarded to the appropriate person.

Usually, local grants are smaller than national grants, and the local manager will only have discretion up to a certain level. For example, when *Ford of Britain* decided to support the Speke Recreation Centre, a leisure centre aimed largely at the unemployed, it offered a grant of £2,000 which was the maximum the Speke management was empowered to give. The project organisers eventually persuaded Ford to give £10,000, but the application had to be referred to the Ford of Britain Trust in Dagenham for decision.

One problem is identifying the ownership of a company linking the local subsidiary to the national company, which might be trading under a completely different name. Two reference books will be useful here, **Who Owns Whom** which is available in most major reference or business libraries, and **Major Companies and their Charitable Support** (published by the Directory of Social Change).

Where a company is contemplating an expansion or a major business development, or a run-down or closure, this can present particular opportunities for obtaining support. For example, *British Coal* and *British Steel* have substantial programmes to assist job creation, training and enterprise in areas of plant closure, and *Eurotunnel* and other major development companies are keen to give support in development areas.

3. Regional companies

There are a number of companies with a restricted geographical area of operation. These will normally confine their charitable support within the geographical confines of their business activity. Such companies might include:

● **Utilities** such as Water Boards and Area Electricity Boards. The privatisation of the utilities will result in much more explicit programmes of community involvement for these companies, many of which will be increasing the funds available for this purpose.

● **Independent television contractors,** all of which confine their giving regionally within their television franchise area, although they do also give to national projects through the Television Fund. Most giving is directed towards the arts and local events.

● **Building societies** all started as small local self-help building clubs. The smaller societies are still locally based, although the larger societies have become major financial institutions with a nation-wide spread of branches. Some larger societies still retain a regional bias or historic links with a particular city. Many have given little in the past except through sponsorship or social lending or the use of branch offices as collecting points. But the Building Societies Association is promoting a stronger community role for societies and has published *Building Societies in the Community* as a guide to good practice.

● Miscellaneous other companies including independent **department stores** (e.g. *Bentalls* in Kingston-on-Thames), independent **brewers** (e.g. *Boddington's* in Manchester), **co-operative societies** (such as the *North East Co-operative Society*), **banks** (such as the *Bank of Scotland*, the *Royal Bank of Scotland* and the *Yorkshire Bank*), **car dealerships**, etc.

4. Local branches

Large retailing companies operate through high street (and shopping centre) branches. Many have a policy of giving small amounts of support to local organisations through these branches. Such support will be given on a direct approach to the branch manager and can be given in cash or in kind or in vouchers. Support will never be large (cash donations will normally be around £25) and the branch manager will have a limited annual budget for the support that can be given.

5. Smaller local companies

In every area there will be smaller, usually privately-owned companies. Some of these will be giving to charity. Some won't. Some might, if approached and persuaded to do so. Their local presence and your local need at least give a good basis for making an initial approach. You can find out about local companies through:

The **local council** which may have produced a list of major local ratepayers (contact Chief Executive's office) or a list of the main local employers (contact the Economic Development department).

The local **Chamber of Commerce**

The **Kompass** register of British industry listed regionally and locally.

Local **telephone directories** of business users (e.g. Thompson Local and Yellow Pages).

Your own **local knowledge** of the area.

The Business in the Community **directory of enterprise agencies** which lists all local Enterprise Agencies and their financial sponsors

A list of the major corporate donors with head offices outside London

SCOTLAND

Bank of Scotland (*Edinburgh*)
Britoil (part of BP) (*Glasgow*)
Wm Collins (*Glasgow*)
Dawson International (*Edinburgh*)

General Accident (*Pithleavis, Perth*)
Grampian Television (*Aberdeen*)
Guinness/Distillers (*Edinburgh*)
Levi Strauss (*various locations*)

Low & Bonar (*Dundee*)
John Menzies (*Edinburgh*)
Royal Bank of Scotland (*Edinburgh*)
Christian Salveson (*Edinburgh*)

Scottish & Newcastle Breweries (*Edinburgh*)
Scottish Television (*Glasgow*)
Stakis (*Glasgow*)

(*Note:* Wm Collins was being taken over by News International at the time of going to press.)

WALES

Laura Ashley Holdings (*Carno, Powys*)   Iceland Frozen Foods (*Deeside, Clwyd*)

NORTHERN IRELAND

Ulster Television (*Belfast*)

NORTH EAST AND YORKSHIRE

National & Provincial Building Society (*Bradford*)
Fenwick Ltd (*Newcastle-upon-Tyne*)
Halifax Building Society (*Halifax*)
Kalon Group (*Batley, W. Yorks*)
Wm Morrison Supermarkets (*Bradford*)
N E Co-operative Society (*Gateshead*)
Northern Engineering Industries (*Newcastle-upon-Tyne*)
Northern Foods (*Hull*)

Persimmon (*York*)
Procter & Gamble (*Newcastle-upon-Tyne*)
Rowntree (*York*)
Shepherd Building Group (*York*)
Tyne Tees Television (*Newcastle-upon-Tyne*)
Vaux Group (*Sunderland*)
Yorkshire Bank (*Leeds*)
Yorkshire Television (*Leeds*)

NORTH WEST

AMEC (*Northwich, Cheshire*)
British Nuclear Fuels (*Warrington, Cheshire*)
Coats Viyella (*Manchester*)
Coloroll Group (*Manchester*)
Co-operative Bank (*Manchester*)
Ferranti International Signal (*Cheadle, Cheshire*)
Granada Television (*Manchester*)
Guardian and Manchester Evening News (*Manchester*)
Kellogg Company (*Manchester*)

Littlewoods Organisation (*Liverpool*)
Alfred McAlpine (*South Wirral, Cheshire*)
Paterson Zochonis (*Manchester*)
Pilkington (*St Helens, Lancs*)
Provincial Group (*Kendal, Cumbria*)
Royal Insurance (*Liverpool and London*)
Tootal Group (*Manchester*)
Trinity International Holdings (*Chester*)
Vernons Organisation (*Liverpool*)

WEST MIDLANDS AND HEART OF ENGLAND

J C Bamford Excavators (*Uttoxeter, Staffs*)
J Bibby and Sons (*Leamington Spa, Warwicks*)
H P Bulmer (*Hereford*)
Central Independent Television (*Birmingham*)
GKN (*Redditch, Worcs*)

Glynwed (*Birmingham*)
IMI (*Birmingham*)
Jaguar (*Coventry*)
Lucas Industries (*Birmingham*)
PMG Investments (*Birmingham*)
J Sackville Group (*Birmingham*)
Waterford Wedgewood (*Stoke-on-Trent, Staffs*)

EAST MIDLANDS

Boots Company (*Nottingham*)
Robert Horne Group (*Northampton*)

Next (*Enderby, Leicester*)
Scott Bader (*Wellingborough, Northants*)

EAST ANGLIA

Anglia Television (*Norwich*)
Fisons (*Ipswich, Suffolk*)
Marshall of Cambridge (*Cambridge*)

Bernard Matthews (*Norwich*)
Norwich Union Life Insurance (*Norwich*)

WEST

C & J Clark (*Street, Somerset*)
Dowty Group (*Cheltenham, Glos*)
DRG (*Bristol*)
English China Clays (*St Austell, Cornwall*)

Television South West (*Plymouth, Devon*)
Westbury (*Cheltenham, Glos*)
Westland (*Yeovil, Somerset*)

SOUTH AND SOUTH-EAST

Berkshire

Bunzl (*Stoke Poges*)
Cliffords Dairies (*Bracknell*)
Hewlett Packard (*Wokingham*)
Metal Box (*Reading*)
Morgan Crucible (*Windsor*)
Nabisco (*Reading*)
Norcros (*Reading*)

Racal Electronics (*Bracknell*)
Ranks Hovis McDougall (*Windsor*)
Reed Executive (*Windsor*)
Siebe (*Windsor*)
3M United Kingdom (*Bracknell*)
UEI (*Newbury*)

Buckinghamshire

Amersham International (*Little Chalfont*)
BPB Industries (*Slough*)
British Alcan Aluminium (*Gerrards Cross*)
Calor Group (*Slough*)
Dee Corporation (*Milton Keynes*)

Food Manufacturers GB (*Slough*)
Johnson & Johnson (*Slough*)
Y J Lovell (*Gerrards Cross*)
Slough Estates (*Slough*)
Wilkinson Sword (*High Wycombe*)

Dorset

McCarthy and Stone

Essex

Ford Motor Co (*Brentwood*)
Plessey (*Ilford*)

Trebor Group (*Woodford Green*)

Hampshire

Eli Lilly Group (*Basingstoke*)
IBM United Kingdom (*Portsmouth*)

Kaye Organisation (*Hartley Wintney*)
Television South (*Southampton*)

Hertfordshire

ASDA Group (*Watford*)
Kodak (*Hemel Hempstead*)
Merck Sharpe & Dohme (*Hoddesdon*)

Smith Kline & French Laboratories (*Welwyn Garden City*)
Tesco (*Cheshunt*)

Kent

Abbott Laboratories (*Queensborough*)
Marley (*Sevenoaks*)

Pfizer (*Sandwich*)
Saga Holidays (*Folkestone*)

Middlesex

Argyll Group (*Hayes*)
Beecham Group (*Brentford*)
British Airways (*Hounslow*)
Courage Group (*Staines*)
Gillette Industries (*Isleworth*)
H J Heinz (*Hayes*)

Hoechst UK (*Hounslow*)
Honeywell Bull (*Brentford*)
Kyle Stewart (*Wembley*)
Rank Xerox (*Uxbridge*)
RMC Group (*Feltham*)
United Biscuits (*Isleworth*)

Oxfordshire

General Foods (*Banbury*)
Oxford Instruments (*Eynsham*)

Sun Hotels (*Henley-on-Thames*)

Surrey

Air Products (*Walton-on-Thames*)
BOC Group (*Windlesham*)
British Car Auction Group (*Hindhead*)
Commercial Union Assurance
(*Croydon*)
Cummins UK (*New Malden*)
Gallaher (*Weybridge*)
Higgs & Hill (*New Malden*)

Johnson Wax (*Camberley*)
Nestle Holdings (*Croydon*)
Redland (*Reigate*)
Securicor (*Carshalton*)
Sterling Winthrop (*Guildford*)
Van Leer UK (*Cobham*)

Sussex

Body Shop International
(*Littlehampton*)

Nissan UK (*Worthing*)

Wiltshire

Allied Dunbar Assurance (*Swindon*)

Burmah Oil (*Swindon*)

Personal links

'Who you know' still remains the most important feature of company giving. Despite the growing professionalisation of the giving process, with many more companies now setting up formal policies and application procedures, many companies still only give to those appeals that concern the Chairman, or Managing Director. Some are quite open about this, whilst others hide behind a non-disclosure of how they spend their charitable budget.

For the well-heeled charity with good connections, life is a lot easier than for the small local perhaps radical or innovative project dealing with an unfashionable or unpopular area of human need. But any charity can develop and use personal contact to further its fund-raising, even though it is harder for some than others.

1. Contacts at the top

Who do you, your colleagues, your trustees or committee of management know who are in senior positions in major companies. Find out, and you may be surprised at the extent of your existing contacts.

But suppose this is not enough. You need to widen your supporter base and to reach out towards companies which have never supported you and where you have no existing contact. What do you do? If you are adventurous, confident and persistent, you might just be able to forge your own contacts. But most would prefer the other option of finding *people who know people* to do the asking.

Many charities launching an appeal to companies first set up a business appeal committee in order to bring together senior business people for the sole purpose of asking for money from their colleagues. The key person to find is the chairman of this committee who may well know of other people who would be happy to give up a certain amount of time for a good cause. The next stage is to list the companies you wish to approach, and arrange that whoever has a personal contact at the top of the company makes the approach either in person, or by telephone, or in writing (in that order of preference).

On a more limited scale, finding someone prepared to write ten or twenty letters for you can be well worthwhile. As an example, the Urban Trust is a charity established in 1987 to generate support for projects promoting the social and economic regeneration of inner city communities. In an appeal prior to launch, a leading businessman agreed to write 20 short personal letters with a simple leaflet on the Trust attached to this letter. This resulted in two donations of £10,000, two of £5,000, one of £500, and three promises of support (unspecified). Not only were the chances of success improved, but the actual amounts that were given were far larger than for an appeal without the benefit of personal contact.

A further idea is to arrange some sort of short meeting to present your proposals to the business community. Such a meeting could be hosted by a leading businessman or some other person with pulling power, or even sponsored by a large company. This can work extremely well for local charities seeking support from local companies, if you can find a way of persuading people to attend.

2. Employee links

Contact right at the top is not the only form of contact which can be used to advantage. Any link between the charity and an employee of a company will be helpful. Given two otherwise identical appeals, the one in which an employee is involved in some way (as volunteer, committee member, in fund-raising, with a family member who has been helped, etc.) is the more likely to be supported. This connection can be mentioned in the appeal letter, or the employee can be encouraged to write the appeal letter on behalf of the charity.

Most companies do say that they give some preference to appeals in which a member of staff is involved. A few of the largest companies have some formal procedure for doing this. For example, many of the banks match the fund-raising efforts of their staff or branches; *Shell UK* has a Community Service Fund to which any Shell employee, retiree or spouse who is involved in an official capacity (e.g. as a trustee) of a charity can apply for a grant of up to £350, subject to the criteria of the fund.

Besides applying to the company for a donation, the employee can be asked and encouraged to ask their colleagues to give support out of their own pockets. The Payroll Giving Scheme introduced in 1987 provides an excellent vehicle for this. Any employee of a participating employer can give up to £240 per annum out of pre-tax income by regular deduction from salary or wages. There is a tax saving of 25 pence in the pound (at 1988/89 rates of income tax), but it is the convenience which makes this really attractive, and for the charity it is the inertia principle that the employee will continue giving until a positive decision is made to stop which will result in a regular and long-term flow of income.

There are two main national payroll schemes: *Give As You Earn* and *Work Aid*. Nearly half the employed workforce of the country are working for employers able to make payroll deductions. There is no doubt that the scheme will expand in scale and importance as a way of giving in the 1990's. The easiest way in is through your existing supporters at their workplace, giving themselves (many donors are happy to give additional support if asked) and asking colleagues (where you may need to supply adequate back up literature). As an example of the potential of the scheme, one charity supporter walked into the local bank branch and the bank teller distributed payroll deduction forms to branch staff with a 100% success rate!

3. Customer – Supplier links

Most charities will purchase supplies from a range of companies: printing, stationery, office supplies, accountancy and audit, legal services, banking, insurance. . . . The providers of these suppliers may well be making charitable donations, and they might be persuaded to help you out of the profits you have helped them earn. The 'big 4' high street banks have traditionally given to a wide range of charitable appeals (via head office to national appeals, with a different procedure for local appeals) on the basis that most are customers, and it has never hindered to point this out when making your application.

Tapping the resources of industry

This article is written by David Irwin, director of Project North East, and first appeared in the 1986 edition of 'A Guide to Company Giving'.

Project North East (PNE) is an independent but non-profit company limited by guarantee, and is recognised by the government as a local enterprise agency. We regard ourselves as social entrepreneurs.

Formally, PNE's objectives are (1) to generate, develop and spread new thinking about job and business creation, maintenance and expansion; and (2) to identify gaps in the existing provision of assistance for job and business creation or in the standards of provision. Put simply, we aim to develop new ideas for business and job generation.

I am conscious that many voluntary organisations do not feature local economic development as part of their work, let alone have it as their priority. Nevertheless, there are similarities in needs. All need to raise the funds, or the alternative resources required to carry out their work and achieve their objectives.

We believe that it is important to work in partnership with both the private and the public sector. Given our objectives it is particularly important for us to be entrepreneurial, innovative, professional, effective and to offer 'value for money'. We have conceived a range of different projects over the last six years; we have devised different ways in which our supporters and sponsors can help us.

We have generally sought more than one sponsor for each project since companies frequently prefer not to be a sole sponsor. That often makes it easier to get the first taker which in turn makes it easier to raise the balance. I can illustrate this with some examples.

An initial grant from *Levi Strauss* enabled us to assess the feasibility of launching a training scheme in North Tyneside. A further grant helped us launch, in 1982, what became one of the first Information Technology Centres, attracting additional funding from Voluntary and Christian Service, North Tyneside Metropolitan Borough Council, the Manpower Services Commission and the Department of Trade and Industry. Levi Strauss accepted a place on the Board. They have subsequently given a further grant to develop specific marketing opportunities. In order to devise a project to help young people start in business, we persuaded *Marks & Spencer* and *Legal & General* each to chip in £1,000 if at least two other companies joined them. In the event, *BP*, *IBM* and *Fenwick's* all helped. This enabled us to produce a prospectus for the Newcastle Youth Enterprise Centre (NYEC). This in turn helped us raise the funding we needed to launch Britain's first Youth Enterprise Centre.

We launched the NYEC specifically to help young people who wished to start their own business. It helps in five ways – by providing counselling support, substantial training, work-space, common services and access to finance.

By the end of 1985, £350,000 had been raised in cash and in kind, 85% of this from the private sector, with around 30 company sponsors supporting the work of the Centre.

We are very conscious of the need to cost our projects accurately and to monitor the time and resources we spend on them, although this is still very difficult.

In order to obtain the support we need, particularly from the business sector, we feel that it is important to project a 'corporate image'; we try to convey an image of what we consider to be our strengths – professionalism, commitment and enthusiasm, a track record of hard work, and an ability to get results fast in the field of local economic development.

We have also taken the trouble to get involved in other organisations where we feel this would enable us to build up contacts and to gain relevant experience. For example, both Managers of PNE are members of the British Institute of Management and the Tyneside Junior Chamber of Commerce. We were both members of the team which won the National Junior Chamber Management Case Study in 1984 and again in 1985. We both decided to study part-time for an MBA at Newcastle, ensuring assignments always related back to the work of the Project. I was Treasurer of North Tyneside Council of Voluntary Service for 18 months; and a member of the Board of a Community Programme Managing Agent for two years.

Why companies get involved

Companies become involved in giving money to charities and to community projects for a variety of reasons. These include a belief that the company should be 'responsible' in the way it carries out its business. As in the US, companies increasingly are aware of the need to satisfy not just their shareholders, but also their employees, consumers, local residents, community groups, etc.

Large companies have been particularly keen to back enterprise projects because they need a healthy small business environment, whether as suppliers and customers, or just because they are a sign of a healthy and growing economy in which to operate. Small companies can provide well trained and more broadly skilled personnel. Some companies, where they are the major employer in a town, feel a particular responsibility to that town, for example *Pilkington's* (in St Helens), *Boots* (in Nottingham), or the *British Steel Corporation* (in the main steel areas).

In 1984, *National Westminster Bank*, for example, committed £4 million – around 1% of pre-tax profits, to sponsorship of charities, sport, and the arts, and to local economic development, and reported that the latter was the fastest growing area of its corporate programme. Sir Hector Laing of *United Biscuits* has actually challenged his big company colleagues to follow widespread American corporate practice and commit 1% of pre-tax profits to the community on a long-term basis.

Legal & General argue that no business can progress in isolation from the environment in which it operates and that a thriving economy provides the best atmosphere for commercial success. It has concentrated on job-creation initiatives because of concern for rising unemployment.

IBM set up its Public Affairs Department in 1967 as a formal recognition that it was no longer enough for IBM to contribute to the economic wealth of the country solely by meeting its basic

117

organisational responsibility. It was felt that it should be participating at another level, devoting resources to help solve problems in society which might appear (to outsiders) quite unrelated
to *IBM*'s basic interests.
The impact the private sector can make is maximised when this
is combined with the public sector, who welcome a private sector
involvement, and the voluntary sector. There is an added bonus
for companies getting involved in these two-way and three-way
partnerships in that it means that their contribution, which might
be relatively quite small, is 'leveraged' to have a much greater
effect. In addition, such co-operation provides a positive and
constructive working together and therefore better mutual
understanding between local authorities, business and the
voluntary sector.

Methods of support

Partnership is becoming something of a buzz word in the field of
corporate support, but it is a growing phenomenon and companies appear fully satisfied with the results they can achieve. It
extends company support beyond simply a cash contribution
(although money is still something they can usefully provide)
into a whole range of other support all of which is useful and
some of which can be provided at little or no cost. It is instructive
to think about how companies can give their support. Perhaps I
can illustrate this with examples from our experience at Project
North East.

1. Cash

● **Grants.** These can be one off or staged. For example, *Legal &
General* agreed to give £10,000 per annum to the Newcastle Youth
Enterprise Centre; four corporate sponsors have agreed to give
core funding to Project North East for a 3 year period to cover our
office costs.

● **Loans.**

● **Loan guarantees.**

2. Manpower

● **Full-time secondments.** Next to cash in importance has been the practice of seconding staff to charities and to local economic development initiatives. Such secondments may be young high-flyers who can benefit from exposure to the wider community, managers in mid-career who are unlikely to be promoted further, or those facing early retirement.

In 1983, Project North East persuaded *Marks & Spencer* to second a young high-flyer, Ian Fisher, to manage our Youth Enterprise Centre. PNE argued that not only was the project worthy of a secondee, but that it was important to have someone capable of setting up and running the Centre and who could relate to young people. We also argued that this assignment would be a good training experience and the secondee would benefit from this involvement.

When Ian returned to M & S we actually interviewed three managers that *British Rail* had offered as suggested replacements for this post. It is very unusual to be given a choice, but this enabled us to replace Ian with another young high-flyer from the *British Rail Property Board.* In addition, BR agreed to give a second person who has become our training manager. *Procter and Gamble* have seconded an administration manager to the Newcastle Youth Enterprise Centre.

It takes a great deal of discussion and negotiation to persuade companies to release their managers on secondment. It is important to approach secondments in exactly the same way as if the position was directly salaried. A detailed job description is needed, together with a 'person description.' Hold an interview, and be prepared to say no if you do not believe the person is right for the job.

● **Short-term secondments.** There is a dramatically increasing demand for secondments, from a whole range of voluntary organisations. Project North East, together with the Newcastle Youth Enterprise Centre, has developed a small but interesting method of boosting help. This has been to arrange a series of short placements, typically of two weeks' duration, often using management trainees. To date *Marks & Spencer, Legal & General* and *Deloitte Haskins & Sells* have all helped in this manner.

Individuals are given a specific assignment with a clear end point, to be completed by the end of the attachment. Placements have researched, written and managed the production of a promotional video for the NYEC; designed a training day on 'Financial Control and Accounts'; investigated the feasibility of a retail outlet for NYEC clients; and much more. Feedback from participants and their companies has been uniformly positive. It is a worthwhile experience, not too long, but long enough to carry out a much needed project for a voluntary organisation. The work provides training and expands the secondees' experience of 'the real world', giving them the chance to use their initiative to reach a specific target without the support system of a large organisation, which boosts self confidence.

● **Part-time secondments.** These can, for example, be one day per week to carry out a specific task such as keeping the books, or occasionally as the need arises. They can be inside office hours or outside. At the Newcastle Youth Enterprise Centre we have devised a way of recruiting people who are willing to give us help and tapping this goodwill when we need it.

To provide help to clients of the NYEC, we have persuaded a number of professional people, such as marketeers, advertisers, accountants, solicitors, architects, graphic designers, etc. to become '*Friends of the Youth Enterprise Centre*' to give advice on an occasional but free basis.

We think of the Counsellors who work for the NYEC as providing a 'general practice'; the Friends are the 'consultants'. So far, about 50 people have volunteered to become Friends and most have been asked at least once to help. Examples of help include preparing text and logo for an advertising leaflet; valuing a shop; reviewing accounts; advising on a partnership agreement; etc. Indeed, now the Newcastle Law Society are providing a fortnightly counselling service at the Centre.

Creating a Friends organisation along these lines is something that anyone could do. It makes great sense because it provides a pool of committed support when you need it. Also it is hard to be refused when you are asking for support in the abstract, and then hard for someone to refuse a specific assignment when they have already volunteered to help.

● **Help on Management Committees.** Company personnel have a major role to play by becoming involved on management boards. For example, John MacCarthy, then Community Affairs

Manager with *Legal & General*, agreed to become the Chairman of the Newcastle Youth Enterprise Centre and was, as such, also co-opted on to Project North East's board. During 1985 he came up for four board meetings and the official opening of the Centre. He usually stayed overnight and spent part of the day outside the board meetings allowing us to discuss further ideas with him. This sort of involvement is also helpful in encouraging other companies to become involved.

● **Access to company's outside specialists.** This is another way of giving particular help that may not otherwise be available. For example, *Legal & General's* marketing agency helped with early PR of the Youth Enterprise Centre.

● **Other access to specialists.** Working with *Bass Riley Design Consultants* in 1985 we developed the 'Design for Enterprise Scheme'. Bass Riley persuaded 9 of their competitors to join with them in offering 10 hours creative time to each of 10 businesses started by young people. If the businesses were paying for the help they received it would have cost them well over £1,000 each.

The *North Eastern Co-operative Society* has a 'social dividend', part of which is used to keep prices low in the shop but part is used for projects in the community. They provided funding to launch Associated TV, a video studio facility at Teesside Polytechnic. NECS agreed to ask Associated TV to make a promotional video for the NYEC at no cost to ourselves.

3. Facilities

● **Conference rooms/training centre.** *BP* have provided facilities for us in London to hold meetings and to make a presentation to big companies.

● **Places on training seminars.** The marginal cost of placing additional people is likely to be low. For example, we have been able to negotiate places on *Post Office* Direct Mail seminars both for our staff and for clients.

● **Printing.** The *Leeds Permanent Building Society* is printing our Youth Enterprise Resources Bank. *ICI* are usually happy to print our annual reports, etc. Many large companies have in-house printing facilities and this is something they can often make available.

4. Donations in kind

● **Discounts.**

● **Equipment.** We have equipped our office and the NYEC almost entirely with discarded office equipment and carpets. The *Trustee Savings Bank* and *Marks & Spencer* were particularly helpful.

● **Travel and Accommodation.** In January 1986, we took 14 people down to London to look for business ideas. We were able to persuade *British Airways* and *British Rail* to provide the travel and *Thistle Hotels* the accommodation. Obviously, if you have an existing contact with a company it becomes easier (and much more cost-effective) to negotiate such in-kind donations than if you have to start from scratch. You know who to approach and they know you.

5. Premises

● **Provision of space.** This can be free office space for your work or your projects. Or it could be space to advertise what you are doing. For example, several building societies and hotels have agreed to give window/display space to NYEC clients. In addition, we had the use of Newcastle Central Station's old information office for six months while it was empty.

6. Total support packages

These different methods of support can often be wrapped up together in one package. For example, one of the smaller firms supporting the Newcastle Youth Enterprise Centre is *Greggs the Bakers*. They looked at all their resources and asked how best they could maximise their commitment. As a result, in addition to making a straight cash grant, they give us access to their mainframe computer, they provide a board member, and the use of their Finance Director for a day a month. Other staff are getting involved as volunteer 'Friends of the YEC' to provide help and advice to individual young entrepreneurs.

Companies are often very keen to supplement their direct cash support with some form of sponsorship. In 1984–85 we persuaded the *North Eastern Co-operative Society* to sponsor the Livewire Awards Scheme in the North East. Beyond giving cash support, however, they actively looked for other ways to bring the resources of their business to bear on Livewire. We borrowed their special events caravan for a Livewire Roadshow to tour Northern towns; their advertising department produced additional publicity material and their Public Relations Division helped with media coverage. Every Co-op store and Co-op Handibank had Livewire displays and entry forms; and staff of the Society acted as Mates to Livewire entrants.

Their support carried into the autumn of 1985 when they agreed to provide nearly half the cost of staging 'Youth Enterprise '85', an exhibition specifically for young self-employed people to exhibit their products and services.

Returns for contributors

Most companies will have specific criteria which they use in choosing which projects to support. These are likely to include geographical location; subject area; potential for leverage; degree of innovation; replicability; scope for direct involvement; track record of the organisation; scope for PR; etc. In addition they may make their donations only to certain legal entities (such as charities).

But what are companies looking for from these contributions?

In its R&D or advertising or production budgets, a company is looking for value-for-money to get the maximum return for each pound spent, although it will not always be possible to gauge accurately the effect of a specific advertising or R&D spend. The sense of value for money is not always present in their community involvement budgets. Sometimes there seems to be a feeling that such expenditure is, per se, beneficial irrespective of where it goes. Or that having committed a certain budget, it does not really matter how it is used up. Other companies, particularly some of the larger companies, are becoming aware that this part of their budget needs to be managed in precisely the same way as other parts of their budget. There should be some sort of overall objective, and there should be some return (not necessarily for the companies) in spending the money.

For example, *Legal & General* looks to support projects which are: (1) making people economically active; (2) have a bias to young people; (3) are geared to meeting demonstrable demand;

(4) are innovative; (5) have competent local management; (6) lever public sector cash with private sector support; (7) have the support of several companies and organisations; and (8) enable funds to be provided in a tax-efficient way. It currently gives particular emphasis to London, Northern Ireland and the North East of England.

As companies themselves become more professional in their approach to giving, they will inevitably look for professionalism in the initiatives they decide to support. They will also be watching to see what impact a project has – not just locally but further afield. For example, there are many Youth Enterprise Centres springing up around the country, frequently modelled on the Newcastle Youth Enterprise Centre.

Another factor they will take into account is how far they can make their money go. If initial grants can lever substantial extra support, from either the private or public sector, then this will always be helpful. For example, *Levi Strauss* now insist that they are in a consortium when they back a project.

Companies with well-established programmes for corporate social responsibility allocate their support on the basis of a proven need. Some more recent converts, however, can be over-concerned with having 'their' project – of being able to claim ownership of something new – even if starting something new is less beneficial to the local community than the upgrading of an existing initiative.

National Westminster Bank now speaks of looking and seeing what does work, because they see too many projects which are cutting across each other. They argue that there is a need to spread more awareness of just what works in the field of local economic development. A similar concern is being expressed by many other major firms – it is all very well to let a thousand flowers bloom in local economic development – but there are dangers of re-inventing the wheel, duplication, and poor quality delivery. Most companies are keen to avoid this.

Lessons

● **Identify your audiences,** the different people who you need to communicate with. It is important for voluntary organisations to remember that they have several 'publics'. Commercial companies generally have one public, that is, their customers. But voluntary organisations have several interested parties to satisfy. We have identified the following main publics for the Newcastle Youth Enterprise Centre:

Potential customers, that is those wishing to start in business

Intermediaries, such as Careers Officers, who might introduce potential clients

Sponsors and supporters, and potential supporters

Organisations and companies interested in replicating the Youth Enterprise Centre concept

Helpers such as Friends and volunteers.

Once your target audiences have been identified, only then is it possible to develop a suitable marketing strategy.

● **Have a work plan.** Firstly, this will impress corporate sponsors. Secondly, and more importantly, they may not like the project for which you are seeking help, but another you are involved with may catch their eye. This happened with Tyne Tees Television, when we approached them for help with our 'Business Bus' – we ended up running the 'Commercial Break' business competition with them.

● **Be wholly professional** in your operation, so that sponsors can see that any money will be well and effectively spent.

● **Make a list of non-financial needs** which you can also discuss with potential sponsors and supporters.

● **Work hard to convince companies to stick with initiatives** for reasonable lengths of time and not to keep rushing off to start new things. In the field of local economic development, for example, companies and others have done the relatively easy jobs of starting local enterprise agencies – the test will come in making these work and prosper.

● **Think of the wider picture** of which you are just a part. I think it is important to have a perspective of what you are doing and what you hope to achieve, and to understand how this fits in with what others are doing, and how it relates to the problems you are attempting to deal with. We see the small-scale employment initiatives we are concerned with as only one part of a wider employment strategy, which involves everyone. It is not just the government which needs to act. Industry has a major task in repackaging jobs to fit the hours and needs of husband and wife in a fast-changing society. And the unions too have to review their role and approach to permit new jobs.

Many of the initiatives in local economic development, 'part-time working' and temporary job creation are frankly micro-employment measures during a period of massive social and industrial transformation. They are designed to demonstrate a practical caring, and to help people to make the transition. They are a helping hand for those not helped by the invisible hand of market forces. Taken individually, they are marginal. Taken together around the country, they become economically as well as socially significant.

David Irwin
Project North East

PART III
CASE STUDIES

Introduction to case studies

In this section we focus on the community involvement policies of four large companies.

Bass is a major brewing and leisure company with a well-thought out programme of donations, sponsorship and employee involvement. With its many retail, hotel and public house outlets it is in an excellent position to encourage contributions from its customers, which amount to five times the total that the company itself contributes in cash and kind.

J Rothschild Holdings is a financial services and investment company, with little contact with the public, run from offices in the West End of London. The donations are handled by the PA to the Chairman and decided by a small donations committee of senior directors. In 1986 the company decided to increase its charitable involvement considerably, and unusually it sought shareholder permission to allocate £250,000 per annum for this purpose. At the same time it instituted a carefully structured donations programme to focus on themes of special interest, local appeals, directors interests and general charitable appeals. Many of the points in the article on *Developing a Corporate Community Affairs Programme* written from the experience of the Allied Dunbar Assurance company were incorporated in the J Rothschild programme (Sir Mark Weinberg, the Chairman of Allied Dunbar, is also a Director of J Rothschild Holdings).

Pilkington is a large industrial company based in St Helens with smaller plants in other industrial centres. As the major employer in St Helens which, like other local industrial companies, has reduced its workforce considerably over the past 15 years, Pilkington is obviously concerned with the well-being of the local community. This is where it concentrates its resources. The company feels that the greatest contribution it can make is through the provision of professional skills, rather than by making cash donations. Pilkington established the first Local Enterprise Agency (the Community of St Helens) and has been a leading advocate of Business in the Community.

Woolworth Holdings (in March 1989 the name was changed to **Kingfisher**) is a holding company operating several retail chains including Woolworth Stores, Comet, B and Q, Superdrug and Charlie Brown's Autocentres. Of the four companies featured in this section, it has the least developed community policy. Mostly its contribution is confined to cash donations, which are made at head office, but also through subsidiaries and local branches. If anything, this example shows how little money is actually available from a large company, and how many locations within the company it is possible to approach to get support. Despite the smallish number of donations made by Head Office, the company does have a donations policy and produces a set of guidelines. But the administration is undertaken by the Company Secretary as just a small part of his duties.

Although these four examples illustrate some of the different approaches to company community involvement and charitable giving, each company is 'unique' in how it sets about the task of applying resources for good causes. Approaches range from *Shell, BP, IBM, Barclays, NatWest* and *Marks & Spencer* at one end of the scale, who maintain large professionally staffed community affairs departments, to *Wilkinson Sword* at the other end, which sees charitable giving as peripheral, so it puts all appeals into a hat and picks out four which receive a substantial donation. Some companies, like *BTR*, believe that contributing in the community is not a proper application of shareholder funds, which shareholders can perfectly well do themselves out of dividends they receive if they are so minded. Some, like the various *water boards* and *electricity boards*, mostly give little or nothing now, but following privatisation are likely to develop substantial and effective community involvement policies.

Company	Bass	Pilkington	J Rothschild	Woolworth
Turnover (£)	3,743 m	2,333 m	n/a	2,172 m
Pre-tax profits (£)	448.6 m	302.3 m	100.9 m	147.2 m
Total community contributions (UK) (£)	1,000,000	2,128,000	250,000	600,000+
Charitable donations (UK) (£)	473,913	195,000	250,000	300,000+
Year end	30.9.88	31.3.88	31.3.87	31.1.89

Bass plc

About the company

Bass is a major company with interests in brewing, drinks, pubs, restaurants, hotels, betting, leisure services. Its main beer brands are Bass, Toby, Worthington, Allbright, Charrington, Tennent, Carling, Lamot, Stones, Barbican. It has the UK franchise for Coca Cola and 7-Up. Its soft drinks include Britvic Corona, Canada Dry Rawlings, Tango, Quosh. Wine interests include Hedges & Butler and Colman's of Norwich (with brands such as Veuve du Vernay, Mateus, Mouton Cadet and Eisberg), the Augustus Barnett retail chain and Toby Restaurants. Hotel interests include Holiday Inns International, Crest Hotels and Toby Hotels. Leisure activities include amusement and music machines and bingo and betting operated under the Coral name. In 1988, Bass sold its holiday and travel business. In the year ended 30 September 1988, the company had a turnover of £3.7 billion and pre-tax profits of £448 million.

Community contributions

In 1988, Bass donated £473,913 to charities. It estimates that its gross contribution to the community totalled nearly £1 million, which includes staff secondments made to charities and other non-commercial organisations. In addition, the company estimates that staff and customers have raised over £5 million for charitable and community projects for local and national organisations.

Charities

The largest donation was £38,413 to the Licensed Victuallers National Homes.

£285,000 was donated at the Head Office through the Bass Charitable Trust. Over 100 individual charities were supported.

A further £150,000 was distributed independently of the Bass Charitable Trust by operating companies within the group.

Typical grant size ranges from £250 to £15,000 on a national level to £100 to £2,500 on a local level. In 1988, a particular effort was made to support hospices, and 7 received donations ranging from £5,000 to £25,000. The company does not support advertising in brochures, purely denominational appeals, local appeals outside areas of company presence or appeals from individuals.

An Appeals Committee which meets quarterly considers requests sent to Head Office.

Employee and customer fund-raising

Bass gives preference to projects where a member of staff is involved and encourages fund-raising by staff and through its many outlets. Examples of successful fund-raising activities in 1988 included:

A tanker driver from Cardiff, himself a former cancer sufferer, raised £6,000 for cancer research. Coral Racing staff raised £1,000 for Birmingham Children's Hospital, Preston Brook Brewery staff raised £2,340 for Comic Relief, and Crest Hotels staff raised £20,000 for a selection of major appeals.

Fund-raising efforts by retail outlets are and always have been a feature of the clubs and pubs trade. Coral Social Clubs customers contributed £45,000 to the British Heart Foundation, Toby Restaurants raised £32,000 for Comic Relief and substantial sums for the ITV Telethon, Customers of 55 Mitchells & Butlers pubs contributed £22,000 to the Coventry Evening Telegraph Charity Appeal for children. The individually managed and tenanted outlets were also active in raising money.

The arts

Bass is an active supporter of the arts. Support is given to major orchestras including The Philharmonia, City of Birmingham Symphony Orchestra and the Halle Orchestra, and to the Birmingham Hippodrome, Sadler's Wells Ballet, Leeds Playhouse and the Royal Academy. Sponsorship by Bass includes the Scottish Fiddle Orchestra, Glyndebourne Opera, Welsh Opera, jazz festivals in Birmingham and Cardiff, brass band festivals in Yeovil and Blackpool, a rock festival on Capital Radio and the Tennents Live! rock music programme in Scotland, folk and country music in Letterkenny and Scotland. Other sponsorship included the Harehills Dance Umbrella in Leeds, the Young Vic fringe theatre awards, and a Shakespeare production at the Edinburgh Festival.

Community awards and joint ventures

Community award schemes provide good publicity for the sponsor as well as support for deserving local causes. They also focus on the pub as a central constituent of active community life. Bass has also undertaken a member of joint ventures or partnerships to promote employment or improve the environment.

The Bass Mitchells & Butlers Young Achiever Award scheme offers financial awards to selected students to help further their careers. Its Community Care Awards were given in 1988 to such organisations as the North Staffordshire Bereavement Care Scheme and the Castle Donington Day Care Centre.

Bass North's Community Awards were given this year to 21 recipients. Major awards were given by Bass Yorkshire to the Vale Centre Community Association at Cornholme, by Bass Lancashire to the Disabled Drivers Voluntary Advisory Service in Carnforth, by Bass North East to the Millfield Community Projects at Whitby, by Bass North West to the Family Contact Line at Altrincham, and by William Stones to the Grimsby and District Paramedic Equipment Fund.

Bass North also made the second of three annual donations to the Halton Development Association, to help promote new industry and commerce in Halton District, home of the Preston Brook Brewery.

Charrington and Company teamed up with the Docklands Community Programme agency to form a joint Community Enterprise venture. The company donated a disused building to provide workshops where the Agency will offer up to 100 places on projects designed to help reduce long term unemployment in Tower Hamlets and Docklands. In one such project, redundant furniture is being restored for those in need.

Charrington also sponsored the planting and aftercare of 1,500 trees for London to help replace those lost in the gales of October 1987.

Tennent Caledonian contributed towards the cost of constructing Glasgow Cathedral's new Visitor Centre. Wellpark Brewery is adjacent to the Cathedral and has long been associated with it. The Tennant's Community Award, worth £3,000 a year, and given to worthy organisations or projects, this year went to the community-run Dean Tavern in Newtongrange.

The Bass Ireland Community Award for 1988 was won by the Ulster American Folk Park in Omagh, County Tyrone, in recognition of its contribution to tourism.

The Bass hotel companies Crest and Holiday Inns International make a contribution principally through their individual hotels. Such contributions range from the provision of free office accommodation for a hospice appeal to various fund-raising efforts for UNICEF by the 30 hotels in Holiday Inns International Asia-Pacific Region.

Hedges & Butler in 1988 launched the Cognac Otard Achievement of the Year Award, to recognise and celebrate achievement in its broadest sense. The awards were presented by Sir Brian Rix on behalf of MENCAP at a charity evening at the Grosvenor House Hotel.

Young people, training and enterprise

Bass is an active participant in YTS training and also is involved in a number of schemes to strengthen links between schools and industry and it provides work experience opportunities for schoolchildren.

Bass is a member of Business in the Community. It supports a number of local Enterprise Agencies and gives financial help to organisations such as Project Fullemploy and the Action Resource Centre. It supports the Youth Business Initiative Scheme in Yorkshire where it has seconded a senior executive as co-ordinator. Bass Mitchell & Butlers has two senior directors seconded to the Prince's Trusts.

Pilkington plc

The company is a major producer of glass and related products worldwide. It employes 57,400 people, of which 14,000 are employed in the UK. The company is based in St Helens where it employes 6,000. Other major UK locations include St Asalph, Glasgow and King's Norton. Subsidiaries include: Triplex Safety Glass Co, Andrewarthea, Barr & Stroud, Chance Brothers. These are in addition to subsidiaries trading under the parent company's name.

A company in a company town

To many, Pilkington and St Helens are synonymous, and as with other company towns, it is a truism that what is good for Pilkington is good for St Helens.

However, this is less true now than in the past, despite the fact that Pilkington has had its headquarters in the town for over 160 years.

Fifteen years ago, Pilkington employed 17,000 people directly in St Helens, approximately one-third of the working population, and indirectly was a major source of income to many others such as suppliers, shop keepers, etc. The company provided the major sports facility in the town, employed several of the stars of St Helens' Rugby League Team, ran the only theatre, provided most of the councillors (it was a rare event when the Mayor was not a Pilkington employee), and the company welfare department looked after about one third of the pensioners in St Helens.

From 1975 the company began to shed jobs. In 1975 a factory making glassware for TV employing some 2,000 employees was closed down. Many employees were transferred to other jobs, but the company suddenly stopped recruiting, and unemployment doubled in St Helens from 4% to 8%. Since 1975 a further 8,500 jobs have been shed, and Pilkington now employs just over 6,000 people in St Helens. Other companies – particularly the 'other' glass companies in the town, United Glass and Rockware – were also reducing their workforce. From 1975 to 1987, over 20,000 people (virtually 40% of the working population) were made redundant in St Helens.

This is as savage a cut back as has been experienced by virtually any town in Britain, but it was mitigated by the fact that the job losses were spread (partly because Pilkington itself, quite deliberately, spread its action over a period of years), and by the fact that Pilkington took action to manage this change. Under the guidance of the then Chairman, Sir Alastair Pilkington, Pilkington decided to try to involve the whole community in the problem, rather than just taking responsibility for the Pilkington part of the problem.

Developing a community involvement in St Helen's

First, Pilkington took the lead in establishing the Community of St Helens Trust which was the first local Enterprise Agency. The Trust has helped over 800 businesses start up in St Helens in the past 10 years. These businesses now employ approaching 10,000 people. The Pilkington contribution is in kind. Apart from a small Government grant available to all Enterprise Agencies, and a number of small donations, the St Helens Trust is never given cash support. The Pilkington contribution ranges from the time given by the Pilkington Chairman, as Chairman of the Governors, to secondment of people, including the present Director of the Trust and his Secretary, the provision of accommodation, telephones, stationery etc. The Trust depends, absolutely, on this support. It will only be forthcoming if the Trust continues to do a good job. This is a virtuous circle. It is also 'virtuous' in that all members of the community can – and do – contribute their skills and expertise.

Following the establishment of the Trust, Pilkington has developed a whole range of other community activities – Youth Training, currently involving 600 youngsters, but now beginning to decline; provision of small factory space; provision of venture capital (when it was not as widely available as it is now, although it still is needed in smaller quantities); running a major Community Programme and now being involved in the Employment Training programme. All of these activities are run by managers from Pilkington on free loan.

The community involvement programme in St Helens is run by Peter Shepherdson, and Pilkington is also involved in a wider context through Business in the Community. There are 8 people in St Helens involved in these activities; most are managers and several quite senior. The total cost to Pilkington is about £300,000 per annum.

Charitable donations

Headquarters is also responsible for a sizeable budget for the more conventional charitable giving. The Grants Committee which is made up of senior managers, not directors, responds to a wide variety of appeals, mostly from local organisations – ranging from scout groups to churches and pre-retirement clinics, the company will also respond to certain national appeals, or to support for the establishment of a Professiorial chair. Pilkington usually responds only to appeals that have some relevance to the business, or to the region – support for the Tate in the North is an example of a regional grant.

Alongside the support that Pilkington plc gives, there are a variety of Trusts established by several generations of the Pilkington family, some quite recently. These are not part of the Pilkington company activity. Although they operate independently of the company, there is a considerable amount of informal collaboration between the trusts and the company to avoid duplication of support.

The Pilkington contributions total

Alongside the HQ activity, Pilkington also expects its divisions and subsidiary companies to be active, and provides budgets for this, not only in St Helens but elsewhere in the UK, and increasingly worldwide. The company is a founder member of the Per Cent Club, committed to giving not less than half-a-percent of pre-tax profits, with a target of one per cent. In the UK, Pilkington spends over 1% of its UK profits, and comes close to this figure on a world-wide basis.

Future trends

The overriding urgency of job creation is diminishing. Unemployment is still high in St Helens, about 14%, but it is coming down and demographic changes will have a further major impact on this trend over the coming years. Pilkington is now able to start thinking of other issues, such as training. The company is also giving attention to the environment; Pilkington has, with others, formed a consortium to redevelop some 40 acres of land next to the Town Centre. This development is under way and will include an hotel to which Pilkington will be a major contributor.

Conclusions

The 1960's and 1970's was a period when industry retreated from involvement in the community. What the 1980's has shown is that companies can make a very real contribution to the communities in which they operate. The Pilkington involvement in St Helens is an example of the change in attitudes and approach. Perhaps it can best be summarised by a reversal of the concept of 'what is good for Pilkington is good for St Helens', to 'what is good for the community of St Helens is good for Pilkington'. The company will continue being involved, but not by feeding more cash to charities. Part of the lesson of Pilkington's experience is that the company contribution will be most effective where it can provide skills, particularly management skills. The best contribution from companies is to offer secondment. Cash will be needed from industry in partnership with others to fund the major projects, such as an environmental improvement scheme, but again involving management partnership.

(This Case Study is based on a talk by Peter Shepherdson given at the Northern Charities Forum in December 1988)

J Rothschild Holdings plc

About the company

The company is an investment holding company with subsidiaries engaged in investment holding, investment dealing, fund management and unit trust management.

The principal UK subsidiaries are: Bishopsgate Progressive Unit Trust Management Company; J Rothschild Capital Management Ltd; J Rothschild Investment Management Ltd; and J Rothschild Securities Management Ltd.

Donations history

In 1986 the company gave £18,000 to charity. But that year, the company decided to establish a substantial and well-planned donations programme and it sought shareholder approval to do this. At the 1986 annual general meeting, a resolution was passed authorising the company to make charitable contributions of up to £250,000 in any accounting period. This has been the allocated annual budget for both 1987 and 1988. As the company is office-based and small (it employed 85 persons, as at February 1989), its contributions are limited to cash support.

In 1987 the J Rothschild Charitable Trust was established as the vehicle for making donations tax-effectively. The trustees (in effect, the donations committee) consist of Jacob Rothschild and Clive Gibson, two directors of the company, and Grizelda Grimond, who is also the Trust's part-time administrator.

Donations policy

At the beginning of each accounting period, a donations policy is established with the aim of donating funds as effectively as possible. In the first two years the annual allocation was sub-divided as follows:

Target areas: 4 themes were chosen in each year, and each allocated £40,000.

Local appeals: A sum of £30,000 was allocated to local appeals for charities working in the West End of London, where the company is based.

General appeals: A sum of £40,000 was allocated for general charitable purposes in response to appeals from staff and shareholders. J Rothschild is the only UK company at present with a stated policy of supporting appeals from shareholders (out of whose funds the donations budget is allocated).

Contingency fund: The balance of £20,000 is set aside each year as a contingency fund to meet requests for support outside these areas. In 1987/88 a grant of £25,000 was made to Save the Children for combating drought in Ethiopia.

Target areas

Each year the Trustees select 4 'target areas', areas of activity which they deem of special merit or urgency, and make major grants, usually ranging from £10,000 to the whole of the £40,000 allocated for the target area, plus some smaller grants.

In 1986/87, 4 areas were: *Relief of Suffering in our cities* (major grants were made to the Prince's Youth Business Trust, the Urban Trust, and the Northern Refugee Centre); *Relief of poverty in the developing world* (£10,000 was donated to each of Hand to Hand, Oxfam, Plan International and the Ryder/Cheshire Home in Nepal); *Relief of drug and alcohol addiction* (grants to ADFAM, Broadreach House, Chemical Dependency Centre, Drugline and Lorne House in Hackney); and *Business education* (grants were made of £30,000 a year to Wadham College, Oxford, for the establishment of a Junior Research Fellowship in Business Education, the first instalment of a 3-year grant, and to Templeton College, Oxford).

The target areas in 1987/88 were: *Mental Health* (major grants to the Richmond Fellowship, the Scottish Institute of Human Relations and the Carr-Gomm Society); *Inner Cities* – the restoration of derelict areas and the relief of problems caused by redevelopment; *Aids for Education Overseas* (included in this theme was continuing support for Plan International which qualified under the relief of poverty lead the previous year); and continuing support for *Business Education*.

This method of allocating funds as major grants in carefully thought out priority areas, rather than giving a much larger number of smaller grants across a broad range of charitable activity, is unusual amongst companies.

Local appeals

The company is based in St James's, off Piccadilly. Although this is a central business district, there are particular problems associated with the area, particularly young people adrift and vagrancy. In the first two years grants were made to Centrepoint Soho night shelter and to St Mungo's Endell Street Hostel, St James's Church in Piccadilly, and the Westminster Advisory Centre. As with target area grants, the policy is to make major grants of around £10,000. In addition £20,000 was given in 1987/88 to the Shared Experience Theatre company for the refurbishment and restoration of the old municipal laundry in Soho for use as an arts and community centre, and smaller grants were made to the Westminster Society and the Piccadilly Advice Centre. A small balance remaining was donated to Kew Gardens for tree replanting.

General appeals

The vast majority of grants made in this category are in the £250–£500 range. In 1986/87, 79 grants were made, and in the following year, 43 grants were made including some larger grants.

Conclusion

This company has organised its giving to achieve maximum impact on limited administrative resources, with clear policies and avoiding the necessity of having to assess 'each appeal on its merits'. The programme is innovative in its style and structure, in its having authorisation from shareholders, in its policy of giving major support to selected local charities and through its openness – it produces a detailed annual report which lists every grant made by the company.

Woolworth Holdings plc

Woolworth Holdings is a major high street and shopping centre retailer. Its operating subsidiaries include: Woolworths plc (Woolworth stores); Comet Group plc (electrical and audio/TV retailers); B & Q plc (DIY retailers); Superdrug plc (drug stores); and Charlie Brown Autocentres plc (motor). It employs a total of 51,500 in the UK. The name of the company was changed to Kingfisher in March 1989, but the operating subsidiary names are unchanged.

Charitable programme

The total donations by the Group were £89,000 in 1987/88. Of this, £54,000 was distributed in grants by Woolworth Holdings, the head office company, with the balance being distributed by the five main operating subsidiaries listed above, each of which has its own separate policy, budget and procedure for making grants and giving support through retail branches. Woolworth Holdings sponsors a number of social initiatives, and B & Q is a major supporter of the Prince's Youth Business Trust. The operating subsidiaries also undertake occasional sponsorship of a promotional nature out of their marketing budgets.

Donations policy of Woolworth Holdings

The policy of Woolworth Holdings is that the main charities benefited by the Company are national charities whose activities are allied to the Group's activities i.e.:

(a) Those relating to the customer base of the operating subsidiaries. This would include charities which benefit children (e.g. homes, relief of poverty and advice) and young families.

(b) Employment schemes which encourage re-entry into employment and wealth generation.

In addition, small sums are available at the discretion of the Appeals Committee (see below) for charities falling outside these categories.

On the choice of project for charities falling within the main categories, the policy is that:

(a) The 'investment' is predominantly in skills and work 'in the field'.

(b) The company's support is for a finite period of no longer than 2–3 years.

(c) Projects are chosen which are well run and will give 'value for money' for the donation made.

In addition the company states that it would like to support 'innovative projects in key problem areas and locations which will encourage more general application subsequently'. The main areas of company support are health/medical, crime prevention, education and enterprise.

The company does not support (a) purely denominational appeals, (b) small purely local appeals, (c) appeals from individuals, and (d) appeals largely for restoration of building fabric. No donations are made overseas.

In 1986/87, out of the £54,000 donated, the largest donation was £25,000 to St John's Ambulance. The previous year a major grant was made to the Anthony Nolan Bone Marrow Appeal.

In 1988, substantial donations were made to: Education 2000 to fund the preliminary BACUP to fund the salary of an assistant Publications Officer; to the Women's National Cancer Control Campaign for research into the efficacy of cancer screening; and to the London Lighthouse Project to fund the salary of a Housing Coordinator. In addition, Woolworth Holdings sponsored the launch of a crime prevention initiative – Crime Concern. With Business in the Community, it helped set up a Women's Enterprise initiative.

Administration of the grants programme

Grants at Woolworth Holdings are decided by an Appeals Committee of the Board which includes non-executive and executive directors. This meets every two months. Appeals are administered by the Company Secretary, Tim Clement-Jones. There is no specialist grants officer or full-time person responsible for charitable appeals. The charitable donations of the operating subsidiaries are smaller, and the person responsible for charitable appeals differs for each subsidiary – the Finance Director, Personnel Director or Marketing Director. Small local support in cash or kind within limited budgets is available through retail outlets. For example, each B & Q Store has an annual allocation of £100, which it can give in one or several grants. Employees have also been involved in fund-raising efforts with the encouragement of their company. For example in 1987, employees of Woolworths and Superdrug raised money for Help a Child to See and The National Children's Home respectively.

Conclusion

The interesting point made by the Woolworth programmes is just how little is available from a large spread out company at any one point in the donations structure, and conversely, how many locations in the company can give support – in Woolworth's case, this is the HQ, five operating subsidiaries, and more than 1,000 local branches. Because of the relatively small sums available and the fact that appeal mail far outstrips the capacity of the company to make grants, appeals need to be clearly matched to the company's interests and presented in a business-like way. Even then, the company cannot respond to the vast majority. In 1986, for example, only 13 grants were made by Woolworth Holdings totalling £39,000 but including the £25,000 to the Anthony Nolan Bone Marrow appeal.

Two other points are worth noting. Firstly, this company unlike most companies with a similar size of donations activity, actually has a policy and publishes guidelines, which is helpful to both the company and applicant charity if these are taken note of. Secondly, the company is moving towards various social sponsorships, such as Crime Concern and the Women's Employment Initiative, where it is more closely involved and to which it contributes more substantially; this support obviously is more closely linked to the company's interests and concerns than its general donations.

In 1988/89, Woolworth's increased its community involvement programme substantially. Charitable donations were in excess of £300,000 (£135,000 of which was donated by Woolworth Holdings) and total community contributions in excess of £600,000.

Developing a corporate community affairs programme

Over the years, *Allied Dunbar*, an insurance and financial services company based in Swindon and now part of *BAT Industries*, has earned a well-deserved reputation as leaders in the field of corporate responsibility. Their influence has been felt in the corporate world generally, with many of the ideas they have pioneered taking root in other companies, and a constant stream of visitors making the trek to Swindon to learn a little of how they set about the business of supporting the community.

The ideas discussed in this article do not represent common practice amongst all companies, but best practice amongst those who take this activity seriously. The ideas are important for charities, enterprise agencies, employment projects and other community initiatives as they represent many of the trends now taking place in the field of company support.

Introduction

A programme may have a number of elements. Most companies will start from cash contributions, and then develop on from those. The other elements will depend upon such factors as the nature of the company, its type of business, the Chairman's preferences, and the views and experiences of the staff who have responsibility for such activities. There are five common recurring areas:

● A cash (or donations) policy.

● Local enterprise development.

● Employee involvement (donations, volunteering and secondment).

146

- Sponsorship.
- Gifts in kind.

There are also secondary or fringe areas, some of which are gaining in importance and these include local purchasing, equal opportunity programmes, and positive redundancy policies.

A cash (or donations) policy

An undefined donations policy considering every request on its merits is usually neither effective for the company nor for the individual charity – as the former spends an inordinate amount of time dealing with applications, and the latter usually only ends up with a small grant which has little impact on its real needs. It is, therefore, desirable to decide upon an agreed policy which limits the range of grants and enables a real impact to be made by the company with the limited amount of resources available. There are three broad aspects to the overall programme, any or all of which may comprise the complete policy.

1. A **special interest** programme: This will enable the company to focus a limited number of quite specific areas. For example, *Allied Dunbar* is involved with community initiatives in Thamesdown, disabled people in the Third World and community care for people suffering from schizophrenia in the UK. Programmes need to run from three to five years to be effective.

2. A **general interest** programme: This involves the company in a limited number of fairly broad areas of interest, which could run for several years or revolve on a staggered basis. This is an approach favoured by *Marks & Spencer* which in their case includes medicine, welfare, the arts and community involvement.

3. **Supplementary policies:** In addition to the special and general interest programmes there are a number of other methods by which a company will be making donations outside the main policy areas. These could include:

- The **Chairman's allocation**.
- **Other Directors' allocations** – which at Allied Dunbar is a nominal £250 per annum.

● **Allocations to branches and regional offices**. This allows for small donations to be made to local organisations in those areas where the company has a presence. At Allied Dunbar, the company's 120 sales branches are given sums of between £60 and £200, whereas British Telecom is more generous in its £7,500 p.a. to each of its 29 regions.

● An **employee matching funds scheme** where employee efforts in raising money or otherwise contributing to a voluntary organisation is matched with cash (this is discussed in the section on the employee as donor).

● Support to **trade charities**.

● **Historical commitments** which have become part of the fabric of the programme, and commitments which a company inherits as the result of a take-over.

Each of these **supplementary policies** will probably have fairly modest budgets compared with special and general interest programmes. They are also likely to follow different procedures and to be dealt with by individuals rather than committees. For example, the Chairman and Directors are not likely to want their allocations to go through the same procedure as the other decisions, preferring instead to have absolute discretion as to how they use their allocation. However, the requisitioning of cheques might best be dealt with by the department responsible for the major policies. This in fact is what happens at *Allied Dunbar*, whereby Directors and Branch Offices make their requisitions to the Community Affairs Department. This enables the department to keep company records up to date (the company is accountable for its charitable expenditure not only to the Trustees of the *Allied Dunbar Charitable Trust*, but to internal and external auditors as well as the Inland Revenue) and gives a discreet opportunity to ensure that the donations comply with charitable law and the company's guidelines (for example, the company would not wish to support an organisation which might harm its image).

Local enterprise development

Many companies now support enterprise development as a

distinct element of their community affairs programmes. The majority confine this to the fairly traditional Enterprise Agency movement which has been successfully promoted by **Business in the Community**, and which is now over 200 strong. This support is primarily through the secondment of staff (estimated at 300 and now accounting for the majority of company secondments in the UK), but can also take the form of direct financial support, as with *BAT Industries*, the parent company of *Allied Dunbar*, which funded Southampton Enterprise Agency in its entirety for the first two years. **Enterprise Agencies** are just one means whereby companies can get involved in stimulating and supporting enterprise development. Others include:

● **Venture capital loan funds** (such as the schemes by *Rio Tinto Zinc*, *Shell* and *Calor Gas*).

● **Support for young entrepreneurs** (the *Shell* Livewire and Young Entrepreneurs schemes being good examples).

● Provision or funding of **work space units** (*BAT*'s work in Liverpool and Brixton is a pioneering example).

● Support to **enterprise training schemes** (such as at *United Biscuits*).

● **Independent employment initiatives** (such as the Coach House in Bristol to which over 20 companies contributed capital costs, gifts in kind and secondees).

● **Publications** (such as *Shell's* 'Creating Your Own Work').

● **Training initiatives** – both the financial support of independent agencies (such as Project Fullemploy), and in-house training via the YTS.

In setting out an Enterprise Development Policy, a company has to decide how to give its support, whether in the form of cash, secondment, management resources and gifts in kind, or the development of small business start-ups, co-operatives and other activities concerned with job creation, including training. It will also have to decide whether to cover the whole of the UK, or give priority to those areas in which the company has a major presence, or to areas of great need such as the North of England. **Business in the Community** provides co-ordination and advice for many companies wishing to get involved in enterprise development.

Employee involvement

Employee involvement can be divided into three broad areas:

● The involvement, with the backing of the company, of individual employees in their work capacity to make available the skills which they use at work.

● The encouragement of employees to give or collect money for charitable organisations.

● The involvement of individuals as volunteers in their own personal right.

The company's publicly stated objectives might be: to encourage all employees (and retirees) to take an active and productive role in their local communities and in wider charitable activities.

1. Secondments (individuals in their work capacity)

There are numerous ways in which employees can use their work skills for the benefit of the community:

● **Full-time secondment** of able staff is a major way that any company can make a significant contribution. Leaders in this field are *IBM*, *BP*, *Marks & Spencer*, *British Rail* and *Midland Bank*.

● **Short-term secondment** of two to four weeks, often using management trainees, is an area of largely untapped potential. Project North East has been particularly effective at attracting this type of secondee.

● **Voluntary job placements** using managerial and technical staff helping as volunteers in their own time is another option. *Allied Dunbar* has set up a scheme known as ALPHA (Allied Professional Help and Assistance) whereby volunteers from the company are taking on specific assignments in their own time for local charities. This is described in greater detail on *page 163*.

● **Assignments.** All companies have many specialists who can be called upon for a once-off task of limited duration, for example, legal advice, design of publicity material, conveyancing, or help with interviews. This is somewhat similar to the ALPHA scheme, but need not be as formalised.

● **Training courses.** A variation is for staff to put on special courses designed specifically for charities. An example is the

Allied Dunbar Marketing Training Department's course on selling techniques for local small businesses which is organised in conjunction with the Swindon Enterprise Trust. *IBM* run a regular week-long residential management training course for charities. *Saatchi and Saatchi* run a one-day PR workshop.

● **The involvement of staff** in the management of local organisations and projects is another option.

2. The employee as donor

The work place is ideal for encouraging individual employees to give of their money and time to worthy causes. The opportunities are many and include:

● Company-led **£1-for-£1 matching schemes**, which are best linked to special events (such as the NSPCC Centenary Appeal), United Nations Special Years (the International Year of the Homeless), or emergency appeals (the Bradford City Football Club fire). It is probably necessary to put a ceiling on the total amount to be matched under any such scheme, but experience suggests this may have to be lifted if staff prove to be exceedingly generous. Companies should be wary of open-ended schemes whereby all donations to any charity are matched by the company, as experience in the USA suggests this approach swallows up more of a company's donations budget than is considered reasonable. The *'Corporate Donor's Handbook'* has a section on matching gifts for anyone who wishes to follow up this subject.

● The whole new potential of **payroll giving**, one important element of which might well be a matching incentive scheme. The leading agency in the field of payroll giving is 'Give As You Earn' which is run by the *Charities Aid Foundation*.

● **Local matching and incentive schemes.** Schemes can also be set up on a local and regional basis with the express purpose of encouraging *group* fund-raising by employees specifically for *local* charities.

3. The employee as volunteer

Recognising individual employees' involvement in charities is common place in the USA, and is ripe for development here. There are two major methods:

● **Support for active involvement.** All employees who have actively been involved (for usually a minimum of one year) in a charity in any capacity would be eligible to apply for a grant for their charity (up to £350 in the *Shell* scheme for their employees and retirees or their spouses who serve on a Committee of Management).

● The recognition of outstanding individual commitment to a limited number of employees each year, perhaps selected by their peers. These **volunteer award schemes** usually involve the presentation of a certificate, a cash contribution to the charity of the winner's choice, a meal or reception with the Chairman, and publicity in the company newsletter.

The company also encourage employees to get involved as volunteers in their own personal capacity, using the work place as a recruitment base. *Allied Dunbar* has a scheme under the heading 'Volunteers at Work', and is using a variety of methods to introduce staff to charitable organisations with the aim of persuading them to get actively involved. Examples of how encouragement is given are:

● Visits to charities during lunch-time or at the end of the working day.

● Bringing charities on to company premises to sell their goods (this works very well with two horticultural schemes for mentally handicapped people).

● Organising fund-raising events for specific local charities, then arranging for the participants to hand over the money or equipment personally.

● Negotiating and offering volunteering opportunities with local charities for as little as a day and as long as a week (four young people recently went as helpers with 10 disabled people on a pilgrimage to Lourdes). *Allied Dunbar* produces a *'Volunteers at Work'* Bulletin to publicise and promote these opportunities.

Sponsorship

Sponsorship may or may not be part of a company's community affairs programme. For some large companies, sponsorship is seen as a purely commercial relationship with a charity and the intention is to obtain pre-planned and significant benefit for the company. On the other hand, *NatWest*, for example, takes a more relaxed view, and often their donations and sponsorship policies overlap. At *Legal and General* sponsorship is located within the Community Affairs Department, whereas with many companies it will be part of public relations for corporate sponsorship, or marketing for brand sponsorship.

Sponsorship has traditionally been confined to support for the arts and sports, but under the leadership of the **World Wildlife Fund**, sponsorship of conservation projects is now well established, and more recently **Save the Children** and **Community Links** have demonstrated that it can be successfully extended to social welfare and community. The first calling point for advice on sponsorship is the **Association of Business Sponsorship of the Arts**. Essential reading includes ABSA's '*The Sponsor's Guide*', and '*Sponsorship*' by Victor Head, who was one of the pioneers of arts sponsorship when at Legal and General in the 1970s. There is also a useful article in '*The Corporate Donor's Handbook*'.

Gifts in kind

For some companies, retailers and manufacturers in particular, gifts in kind could be a major feature of a programme in terms of volume, organisational time and total value. Guidelines on how to dispose of damaged goods, seconds, goods as new would probably be helpful, so as to achieve a consistent approach throughout the company's many outlets. It might help if these were linked to the company's donations programme.

Examples of 'gifts in kind' at *Allied Dunbar* include the donation of computer equipment to special needs schools, the loan of vehicles, the design and printing of publicity material, and the use of premises for special events.

Staffing and management

More and more companies are now realising that it makes good business sense to give adequate thought to their community affairs policies and to back those up with appropriate staffing, location, and decision making.

To staff or not to staff is a key question. The general pattern amongst companies is to hive the work off to an existing member of staff with other responsibilities (usually the Assistant Company Secretary or the Head of Personnel), but increasingly more companies are appointing someone full-time, the appointment usually being made from within. However, there is a lot of merit in having (a) open appointments, and (b) recruiting individuals with a sole responsibility for community affairs. If a programme is to be cost-effective in business terms, if it is to develop, if it is to make the optimum use of the resources at its disposal, and if it is to gain credibility within the company and the confidence of the community at large, then it must in due course appoint competent staff to manage it.

Where within the company this individual or group is based is important. The Chief Executive's office, Public Relations or the Secretary's office seem to be favoured places; but wherever, it is useful to have a direct link to the top.

In due course it might be necessary to create a separate unit or department and pull together all the different activities which have grown up over time. The Community Affairs Department at *Allied Dunbar* is a recent creation and stands on its own as a separate entity. By way of contrast *British Telecom* has a Charities Unit (which was previously in the Secretary's office); secondments are carried out by its Personnel Department; education, sponsorship and enterprise development by the Community Relations Department; and there is a separate Action for Disabled Customers team.

If staff are employed to carry out these activities it is important to have a line management structure. In the case of *Allied Dunbar*, reporting is direct to one of the main Board members.

A clear decision-making structure is essential. Who will make decisions with regard to the donations policy? It is usual to give the Manager/Administrator responsibility for decisions up to a certain amount, then there is often an intermediate stage where the Manager consults with a senior Director, and beyond this will be a Committee stage which deals with all grants over a certain level.

Allied Dunbar also makes extensive use of 'Advisors' (perhaps the only company in the UK and the USA to do so). The use of external advisors in the decision-making process has distinct advantages, not least of which are credibility in the outside world and more effective decision making.

Final comments

These then are some of the key ingredients of a company community affairs programme, much of it based on the activities at *Hambro Life*, now renamed *Allied Dunbar* following the takeover by *BAT Industries*. Experience shows there are two important points to remember when developing a programme. Firstly, nothing happens overnight, and therefore any programme will take time to develop and to mature. Secondly, there is no one model format. Each company has to find its own way, whilst learning from the best of others, taking into account the nature of its business, its 'culture', its own objectives, the amount of resources it proposes to allocate, and of course the changing social environment which it seeks to engage with.

Allied Dunbar has recently tried to list the factors that have contributed to the company's success in developing its community affairs programme. These include:

General

The 'nature' of Allied Dunbar as a company which generates loyalty to its objectives.

The whole policy has been removed from the boardroom.

Employment of staff with sole responsibility (and under open-competition).

The 'style' of the staff.

The use of outside advisors.

A business-like approach to social responsibility.

Concern for 'quality' of giving, not 'quantity'.

An open approach – public reports, documentation.

Flexibility and trying a variety of approaches.

Participation in the local community.

Regular self-evaluation and appraisal.

Not being afraid to learn by mistakes.

The fact that the main objective is the contribution to the community – public relations is ancillary to this.

The company accepts publicity, but does not solicit it.

Staff schemes

Positive company support for developing and encouraging the scheme.

The company absorbs administrative costs.

The company gives the key people 'time-off' to get involved.

The company allows use of facilities.

£1 for £1 matching of employee contributions in early days.

The company lets staff manage staff schemes without interference from top management.

The company has never allowed fund-raising to become routine.

Grants policies and procedures

Simplify procedures, whilst retaining accountability for the expenditure.

One-door procedure (no back-door grants are made on the basis of personal contact).

No deviation from mainstream policies for Board Directors.

The creation of an outlet for Board Directors to give (small) grants at their own initiative.

Clear, well defined policies.

A narrowing down on specific areas.

More money to fewer projects in order to maximise impact.

Policies which run from 3 to 5 years.

Willingness to co-operate with other grant-givers.

Visits by departmental staff to projects.

Flexibility over grants – recurrent, intermediate, matching, loans, starter grants are all made, according to need and circumstances. The company can also react speedily when the need arises.

Backing a good individual; this can be as important as the apparent quality of the project or reputation of the organisation.

Initiating the company's own schemes.

Specific policies

Thorough research before a new policy is launched.

Defining clear objectives and setting targets, with continual monitoring of performance.

Building up of networks of contacts within the specialist area of support.

Volunteering

The company is able to offer a variety of opportunities to its staff.

Run with the individual's interests, and follow up on any ideas which emerge from an individual's involvement.

Recognition or reward for achievement.

Other Activities

The Community Affairs Department is an integral part of the company, not a fringe activity.

The department makes use of the resources of the company for the benefit of charities and the community.

The company gives advice and information that is reliable, in addition to making financial assistance available.

Useful publications

'**The Corporate Donor's Handbook: A guide to good practice in company charitable giving**' by Michael Norton, with additional contributions from Des Palmer, published by the Directory of Social Change, Radius Works, Back Lane, London NW3 1HL (£12.50).

'**Company Support for Charities: Guidelines**', presented by the Council for Charitable Support and published by the Charities Aid Foundation (free).

'**Working Partners**' (some examples of involvement in local community life by businesses and the people in them) by Peter Whates, published by the Volunteer Centre UK, 29 Lower Kings Road, Berkhampstead, Herts HP4 2AB (free).

This article has been written by **Des Palmer** and **Jerry Marston**, Community Affairs Department, Allied Dunbar.

Non-financial giving by Allied Dunbar

In this case study we examine how one company, *Allied Dunbar Assurance plc*, has developed its non-financial involvement within the local community in the Swindon area where it is based. Allied Dunbar is not a typical company. It is the undoubted leader in the field of company community involvement, and unlike most other companies it has a policy for making the resources available, it has an administration system for achieving this (its Community Affairs Department), and it has a desire to do as much as it can. In other areas, the local company may not be so receptive to requests for support, or it may need more persuading before it says yes. However, the example of Allied Dunbar shows the potential for charities to unlock valuable and otherwise costly resources from local companies and other companies who have the required resources.

The text that follows gives details of the non-financial support given by Allied Dunbar. It has been provided by the Allied Dunbar Community Affairs Department and illustrated by examples from their experience. It is not meant as a comprehensive list of every kind of non-financial support, but is illustrative of the range of ways in which support can be given.

Resources and facilities not directly involving personnel

1. Premises

With seven buildings in the centre of Swindon, Allied Dunbar has premises which are highly suitable for use by community groups – a restaurant, interview rooms, lecture theatres, training rooms, etc. The company cannot accommodate organisations requiring a regular meeting place but for a special event it is happy to help. In recent years the company has hosted:

● The launch of a local hospice appeal (The Prospect Foundation).

● The launch of the South West Caribbean Focus (complete with steel drums, African dancers and rum punch).

● Annual meetings of Druglink, an advice and information agency.

● A series of presentations to teachers on identifying child sexual abuse. (These were based around a publication which the company's employees sponsored on behalf of the NSPCC.)

2. Design and printing service

The quality of printed material to a charity is important in creating a professional image both to the people that it serves and to potential grant-givers. Many companies have their own in-house design studios and printing departments and could therefore give an invaluable service at relatively low cost to the company.

The staff in the Allied Dunbar design studio have provided service to local charities for many years. Through the Allied Dunbar Charitable Trust, the company allows the use of this facility to local groups for the purposes of designing and printing headed paper, leaflets, posters and similar small items. This does not result in glossy items that are both costly to the company and in the long term to the charity (as they have to pick up on the costs after the first print run). However, the aim is to provide the highest quality design and print at a level consistent with the standard of company printing. The service is limited to new charities, and to new ventures by existing charities, and generally to one item involving no more than a ream of headed paper (500 leaflets). There is no charge for this service but the printing costs are charged to the Allied Dunbar Charitable Trust. In 1988, 25 separate jobs were undertaken at a cost of £3,000.

3. In-house publications

Many companies produce their own in-house publications, some of which will also be of use to community groups. The Allied Dunbar Personnel Department has produced a series of training manuals including 'The Good Meeting Guide', 'Managing Time Effectively' and 'A Guide to Effective Listening'. These are made available on a selective basis to organisations who might gain some benefit from them. For example, the Listening guide is clearly relevant to such organisations as the Marriage Guidance Council, the Citizens Advice Bureau and the Social Services Department all of which have been given copies.

While on the subject of publications, it is probably worth mentioning the booklet, 'In a World of Their Own', which was written, produced, printed and made available by the company for those looking after confused elderly relatives. Originally meant for people in Swindon it has proved to be so popular that it has been requested by over 200 organisations throughout the country.

4. Furniture and equipment

All companies have secondhand and surplus office furniture (desks, tables, chairs) and occasionally equipment (such as typewriters, overhead projectors and photocopiers). For many years at Allied Dunbar, all furniture items were channelled through the Community Affairs Department for distribution at no cost to local charities. During the 12 years that this facility was provided the company helped to furnish just about every charity in the Swindon area.

Allied Dunbar now has a more ad hoc policy. Good equipment is harder to come by. But whenever there is anything which is no longer required by the company, or equipment which is obsolete or slightly damaged, it is always offered to the Community Affairs Department to see if a home can be found for it. The company has disposed of a printing press, a rather large paper collating machine, and over 1,000 waste paper bins (to local horticultural charities to use as plant tubs). The company rarely, if ever, charges for these items.

5. Scrap materials

Every company has scrap material and offcuts such as paper, cardboard, pallets, paint, cloth – in fact the list is endless. In some areas of the country such as London, Bristol and now in Swindon, there are Scrapstores which are willing to collect these items and re-sell them at a very modest cost to playgroups and to schools. Swindon Scrapstore, which Allied Dunbar helped to set up, now receives much of the company's scrap. Others also benefit. When the company changed its name (from Hambro

Life), it had tons of paper which was still useable, and invited all schools in the area to come along on a given afternoon and take away whatever they could carry.

6. Giving sales access to charities

A large and centrally based company has a workforce which, if it can be reached can become clients, customers or supporters. For the past three years, Allied Dunbar invited Jubilee Gardens and the Fairfield Opportunity Farm, both horticultural charities for people with a mental handicap, to sell their plants to company staff. This they do over a two-hour lunch period, either in the courtyard of the main building if the weather is fine, or in the reception area if it is not. Both these charities have received regular support from the Allied Dunbar Charitable Trust and the Swindon Staff Charity Fund, so it is highly appropriate that the company should be providing a captive market. The handicapped people themselves serve the customers.

At Christmas, the company invites charities in to sell their cards and small gifts. Participating charities have included the Wiltshire Trust for Nature Conservation, the Syd Turner Kidney Appeal and the Prospect Foundation Hospice. Whether selling bedding plants or Christmas cards, this provides charities with the opportunity to earn some money and to advertise themselves, whilst at the same time providing a practical and much appreciated facility for the company's staff.

7. Giving sales access to small businesses

Last year the company extended its service to include new small businesses which have been helped by the two local Enterprise Agencies (both of which are supported by Allied Dunbar). A designer of personal leisureware and a glass engraver were each given the opportunity to sell their goods to our staff during a lunch period.

8. The 'Living with . . .' series

An extension of giving access to charities are the 'Living with . . .' discussions. These are lunchtime sessions, where staff bring their own sandwiches and have the opportunity of discussing particular social issues and problems. This was launched by a member of staff who is himself blind and who uses a guide dog to get about. The session was attended by over 40 people including two main Board Directors. This was followed by 'Living with Mental Handicap' and 'Living with Alcohol Addiction'. The company hopes through this series to provide individuals and organisations with a platform, not primarily to raise money, but to increase awareness and to influence attitudes.

9. Invitation to lunch

For some people, lunch in a Company restaurant may be a major event, even a challenge, as well as a pleasure. Over the past few years Allied Dunbar has invited small groups of people with a mental or physical handicap to lunch. These visits are made as natural and relaxing as possible, and also provide educational experience for staff.

At the annual company 5-A-Side Family Day, guests for the past three years have been wheelchair bound youngsters from the local Shaftesbury Society home.

The direct involvement of employees as professionals and as volunteers

This second broad category in many ways offers the greatest potential for the community and for the company. Allied Dunbar has not yet developed a secondment programme in the traditional sense of full-time external placements, but has found a variety of other ways of making its 'people' available.

1. Trainers and training courses

Allied Dunbar has training departments in Personnel and in Marketing. Places on company courses are occasionally made available to representatives from local organisations. For example, a Time Management course has been attended by a Probation Officer. The company Marketing Training Department has for over three years been running a one-evening course for up to 20 self-employed people under the heading 'Selling Yourself, Selling your Product'. This has also been put on for trainees from Project Fullemploy in Bristol. Trainers have also taken their skills outside the company to run half-day courses on telephone techniques and on time management. Personnel Department staff have been involved in short-listing interviewees for Oxfam and in helping to find counsellors for the Marriage Guidance Council.

In December 1987, the Personnel Department put together a day-long learning programme for the director of a national organisation for disabled people in Zimbabwe. He was in Britain on a three-month study course at the invitation of a Third World charity (Action on Disability in Development), which incidentally Allied Dunbar set up. More recently four members of the Marketing Department hosted a session for women trainees involved in a local marketing project.

2. Senior management and the management of charities

Involvement of senior staff in the management of projects that the company has given financial support to is something that has long been encouraged at Allied Dunbar. For example, the now Deputy Chairman of the Company was for seven years Chairman of Thamesdown Voluntary Service Centre, the Director of Finance is on the Board of Swindon Development Agency and Deputy Director on the Board of the Swindon Enterprise Trust.

3. The 'Alpha' scheme

The involvement of technical, specialist or managerial staff with local community organisations has now been formalised under the company's 'Alpha' scheme (Allied Professional Help and Advice). This was set up at the beginning of 1987. In its first year the scheme involved Accounts, Premises and Systems departments. Six members of Accounts staff helped eight local organisations with a variety of short-term financial matters such as year-end balance sheets, audits, budgets and grant applications. Two Premises department staff advised on the purchase and installation of a new telephone system for a youth training project and helped two others search for premises. Three Systems department staff helped to install computer systems in the Swindon Development Agency, the Citizens Advice Bureau and the Prospect Foundation Hospice. In 1988, seventeen tasks were completed and another ten got underway.

The scheme was set up on the basis that all staff should volunteer rather than be co-opted, that the tasks they undertook would be quite specific and of a limited duration, that it would be a free service and that wherever possible there should be a spin off for the company. For example, the scheme in the Accounts department was set up on the basis of providing practical experience for trainee accountants in skill areas not necessarily connected with their current tasks in the company.

4. The volunteer programme

The Company's Volunteering Programme was also introduced in 1987. It grew out of the involvement of Swindon staff in the management of their own Staff Charity Fund and from fund-raising efforts by individuals and departments. This was formalised into a programme which offers a variety of opportunities for all members of staff to get involved with or to learn about organisations in the local community. The quarterly *Volunteer Bulletin* offers everything from sign language courses, riding water chutes with mentally handicapped youngsters, travelling to Lourdes with handicapped people, visiting the local Accident and Emergency Unit, playing wheelchair handball against physically disabled schoolboys and various sponsored events. It is in fact, as varied a programme of fund-raising, educational and personal involvement events as is possible. In the two years that it has been running, over 500 people have taken part.

This Volunteering Programme is immensely challenging because it offers the potential of involvement by *any* individual, irrespective of his or her skills, status within the company or levels of remuneration, and because the company is able to develop projects around the interests of staff and the initiatives of organisations who would not normally come within its grants programme.

The involvement of the staff of the Community Affairs Department

Although many non-financial services are provided by the Community Affairs Department, the majority of companies do not have a specialist team dealing with charities. There are three broad areas of help given:

- Advice-giving, particularly with regard to fund-raising.
- Personal involvement in the management of charities.
- Personal involvement in charity recruitment.

1. Fund-raising advice service

Over the years Allied Dunbar has been asked by more and more local and also national charities to give advice and information on many aspects of fund-raising. This has now developed into the following:

● A leaflet on sources of funds for small and medium sized charities ('Pennies from Heaven').

● A reference library of over 150 items on fund-raising plus information on the community affairs policies of over 50 UK and USA companies.

● Advice giving by post, telephone and in person, to local and national charities, such as The Canon Collins Educational Trust, Save the Children, Oxfam, the Bristol Community Trust and the 'Charities at Work' Consortium (all helped in 1987).

● Participation in conferences, seminars, events, on topics including general fund-raising and specifically on payroll giving to both local and national audiences.

● Professional help to specific appeals. In 1987, the local hospital's Scanner Appeal was assisted, and in 1980 a great deal of help was given to the Thamesdown Hydrotherapy Pool appeal, including writing a plan of action, drafting an appeal leaflet, arranging for an employee to produce a portfolio of photographs, and persuading two company departments to make this their 'charity of the year'.

All of this advice and information is given without charge.

2. Involvement in the management of charities

Involvement in the management of local organisations is undertaken for one of three reasons; a personal interest, a specific approach from the Trustees, or more often through a direct request from a charity. This has led to active involvement by members of the Community Affairs Department on the management committees of such organisations as the Thamesdown Helping Hand Fund, the Swindon Youth Project, the Wiltshire Rural Initiatives Fund, the Thamesdown Voluntary Service Centre, Age Concern Thamesdown, the Swindon Gateway Club, the Wiltshire Trust for Nature Conservation, the Thamesdown Citizens Advice Bureau, Bootstrap Enterprises, and other local groups.

3. Involvement in charity recruitment

The company's 'community development' approach locally leads its involvement in many selection interviews, invariably for posts which the company is part-funding. Sometimes such involvement is a condition of grant, or it might be at the request of the charity. In 1987, for example, company staff were involved in interviews for two Development Officers for Bootstrap Enterprises, a Money Advice Worker for the Citizens Advice Bureau, the Co-ordinator for the Third Age Project, the Director of the Alcohol Advisory Council and the Premises Manager for the Swindon Development Agency workshops.

The benefits for the company

Company commitment goes a good deal further than the handing over of cheques. Advice and information giving, and personal involvement and support and encouragement in numerous other ways has grown enormously over the years. We feel it represents a valuable additional input to our cash donations.

What the benefits of doing this are to the company is a most difficult question to answer, because it is almost impossible to measure in anything other than broad terms. As a consequence of company non-financial involvement three things happen:

● In making available premises for special events, in providing access to charities and through giving space on training courses, a considerable number of people of all ages and of many different backgrounds are brought into the company. For many people, especially those within the voluntary sector, there still is a degree of ignorance or even of hostility towards the private sector, and getting them into our premises, and bringing them into contact with company staff, helps in some ways to break down these barriers, many of which are fostered by lack of contact and misunderstanding.

● By making available our publications and printing leaflets for organisations, we are taking the company's name out into the community, into organisations and into homes. Through these leaflets, the company becomes associated with a whole range of charitable causes, not all of them ones that evoke immediate public sympathy. In a low key way this provides good local PR.

● When staff go out into the community to volunteer or to take on technical or professional assignments for voluntary organisations, they are creating a very positive image of the company. They are all acting in one way or another as ambassadors.

Through these three ways the image of the company is in part created, or sustained or changed. Hopefully it is an image of generosity, of commitment, of caring and of enthusiasm. Any company needs the support of its local community for at least three reasons – the community provides the company with employees, with clients, and the company must be seen as a good neighbour, since it requires services from many others and it needs to co-exist with a local authority which can hinder or help its operations. How far the activities listed in this article help in the pursuit of these objectives it is extremely hard to measure. But there is no doubt that they do make a positive contribution to the general feeling of goodwill.

There are two other benefits, perhaps easier to measure:

● Staff undertaking tasks for local charities often find there is a direct benefit in terms of improvement in their own experience and skills. For example an accountant has said 'I enjoyed putting my skills to good use, I was surprised to find how helpful the experience was in terms of my own work'. The company is in the process of trying to quantify this in more precise ways with a survey of past committee members of the Allied Dunbar Staff Charity Fund. The aim is to find out in what ways their involvement in managing the Fund benefited them personally and in relation to their work. However, there can be no doubt that involvement with the problems of others less fortunate than themselves makes staff more caring, more concerned and more effective employees, and for those involved in management, better managers.

● Whenever a group of staff work together in aid of a charitable cause, a secondary spin off is invariably an increased sense of group morale and well being. A good example of this was a company 'Breakout' in May 1987 when 120 members of staff, all of whom were in fancy dress, 'escaped' from the main building with the objective of getting as far away as possible in 8 hours without paying for transport or breaking the law. This involved staff from all levels of the company. The 'Warden' who opened the gates and fired the starting pistol was the Director of Finance. This produced a carnival atmosphere and tremendous friendly rivalry amongst the different departmental teams (as well as raising £10,000 for charity). In a company where teamwork pressure and deadlines are everyday features, such activities can only be a good thing.

Written by **Des Palmer,** *Community Affairs Manager,* Allied Dunbar Assurance plc, Swindon SW1 1EL.

Bibliography

A Guide to Company Giving
Major Companies and their Charitable Giving

Two books, with new editions published every other year, to help grant-seekers in their corporate fund-raising. The *Guide to Company Giving* covers 1,300 large companies with brief financial information and details of donations policy where available. *Major Companies* gives in-depth coverage of company structure, business activities, and charitable and community programmes for the top 350 companies. Both are available from the Directory of Social Change, Radius Works, Back Lane, London NW3 1HL.

The Corporate Donor's Handbook

A detailed guide to *all* aspects of company giving including the administration of company donations programmes, with case studies of good practice. Although aimed primarily at the corporate donor, this book gives detailed insight into company giving practice and procedure for the grant-seeker, available from the Directory of Social Change (*address as above*).

Charity Trends
Charity

Charity Trends is an annual survey of charitable giving published each November, and it includes a list of the top 400 corporate donors. *Charity* is a monthly magazine on charitable giving and fund-raising. Both are available from the Charities Aid Foundation, 48 Pembury Road, Tonbridge, Kent TN9 2JD.

Directory of Enterprise Agencies
Business in the Community

The *Directory of Enterprise Agencies* lists every local enterprise agency, with name, address and contact, and also details of all major sponsors (this list provides a useful list of larger local employers with an interest in the community). *Business in the Community* is a quarterly magazine on company community involvement published by Business in the Community. These are available from BIC, 227A City Road, London EC1V 1LX.

Company annual reports

Most companies are happy to supply a copy of their annual report on request. A few of the very largest also produce a special report on their community involvement programmes. The 'Report of the Directors' section of the company annual report will state a figure for the company's total charitable donations. This may be accompanied by an explanation ranging from a few qualifying words to several pages of pictures and text describing the company's community programme. A few companies even list the main recipients of their support. The company annual report will also give details of the company's business activities, a list of directors often with some biographical detail, subsidiaries, figures on profit and turnover and other financial details.

Building Societies in the Community

A report on current practice and ideas for further involvement by building societies. Societies have not (up until now) been at the forefront of company giving, but with their emergence as major financial services organisations and the possible conversion of some to plc status, their involvement in the community is set to increase. This report is available from the Building Societies' Association, 3 Savile Row, London W1X 1AF.

Getting the Best from Secondment

A practical guide to all aspects of secondment, available from the Action Resource Centre, CAP House, Third Floor, 9–12 Long Lane, London EC1A 9HD.

The Sponsor's Guide
Business and Arts Bulletin
ABSA Annual Report

Three useful publications from the Association for Business

Sponsorship of the Arts. The first is a practical guide to all aspects of sponsorship. The second is a quarterly magazine. The ABSA annual report details ABSA members and patrons and the sponsorship activities of many of these member companies. All three are available from the Association for Business Sponsorship of the Arts, 2 Chester Street, London SW1X 7BB.

E C Eye: Employee Community Involvement

The quarterly magazine on employee volunteering and the involvement of company staff in the community, available from the Volunteer Centre, Lower King's Road, Berkhamsted, Herts HP4 2AB.

Directory of Directors
Who Owns Whom
Kompass Register of British Industry
Times 1000

and other business guides and directories to be found in reference and business libraries.

Action Match

This project, established in 1989, seeks to encourage business sponsorship for good causes and local projects. For details of information available, contact Action Match at Community Links, 81 High Street South, London E8 4EJ.

Covenants
Tax and Giving Subscription Service

Two tax guides which include detailed section on tax-effective company giving. Both are available from the Directory of Social Change (*address as above*).